CU00496761

Beyond Coping
Finding Your Way Forward

Beyond Coping
Finding Your Way Forward

Bring about changes you want
during and after
the COVID-19 pandemic

Ben Scott, A. Biba Rebolj and Greg Oberbeck

BT Press

First published February 2021

© Ben Scott, A. Biba Rebolj and Greg Oberbeck 2021
sfpossibilities.org

Illustrations by Nick Ellwood
nickellwood.co.uk

Designed by Alex Gollner

The characters in this publication are fictional creations.
Any resemblance between these fictional characters and
actual persons, living or dead, is purely coincidental.

No part of this publication may be reproduced, stored in
a retrieval system, or transmitted in any form or by any
means, electronic, mechanical, photocopying, recording or
otherwise without the prior permission of the copyright
owners.

Published by
BT Press
17 Avenue Mansions
Finchley Road
London NW3 7AX
(020) 7794 4495
btpress.co.uk
orders@btpress.co.uk

ISBN 978-1-871697-80-3

CONTENTS

For
Thelma and Michael,
characters in my life story for whom
I will always be grateful.

Ben

For
my nephews, Mani and Nick,
who are becoming both passionate
readers and persistent joggers.

Biba

For
Mom and Dad,
for your unwavering support
and encouragement. Without you,
I would not be who I am today.

Greg

FOREWORDS

The authors of *Beyond Coping* must be congratulated on their brilliant idea for a self-help book for these challenging times. Taking the radical and effective counselling model known as Solution-Focused Brief Therapy, they have adapted the concepts and techniques of this approach into a story in which the characters use Solution-Focused questions as part of everyday conversations.

The reader is taken on a journey with the central character, the Jogger, as she deals with the fears and anxieties we all recognise in the pandemic era. The story develops beautifully, and every page contains gems of wisdom; a favourite of mine is the idea of the 'inner backpack'.

The clarity of the writing will give professionals already acquainted with the Solution-Focused approach many new ways of constructing useful conversations with those they work with.

Primarily, though, this book will be of tremendous help to so many struggling with uncertainty and stress, and the lessons it delivers are relevant to the way we manage our lives now and in the future.

Harvey Ratner,
co-founder of BRIEF

The pandemic has challenged us all in so many ways. As well as exacerbating our worries for our mental health, the restrictions of lockdown increase the risk that our hopes and dreams will fade as we struggle to find ways of dealing with the impact of COVID-19. This book offers an alternative, inviting us to look to the future and to celebrate what we are doing that is working, to focus on our capabilities rather than our failings. *Beyond Coping* is born out of a particular time, but its valuable guidance will be just as applicable when the pandemic is history.

Evan George,
co-founder of BRIEF

INTRODUCTION

COVID-19 has changed the world. We have seen this through restrictions in travel, our children's education, our ability to work and socialise, businesses closing down, and having to wear masks in shops and on public transport. While there are certain aspects of the pandemic that have affected everyone, each of us will have our own unique story around this.

While under various lockdowns and restrictions, many of us will have experienced a great sense of loss – loss of loved ones, loss of freedom, loss of independence, loss of work. The list goes on. Because of these losses, many of us have felt isolated, discouraged and hopeless, which is understandable given the unprecedented changes we are living through.

Most of us have found that our opportunities for social interaction have drastically reduced. The thought of meeting up with friends, attending sporting events or spending time at the beach or in a park is now filled with doubt and caution. We're constantly watching everyone around us to check how close they are and whether they're wearing a mask.

This also means that when we try to support others our ability to do so has changed. We haven't been as free to meet for a cup of tea or a pint in the pub; it hasn't been as easy to visit friends and family;

and we've often not been allowed to give our loved ones a hug.

So what are we left with? What is still present for us? Our time to reflect and our ability to talk to each other. We can still speak on the phone, send text messages and have video calls: we have remained connected. It is these conversations that can make a profound difference in such challenging times, when we're trying to grasp some sense of normality.

In this book we're going to explore a day in the life of a 'Jogger' via a series of conversations. The Jogger is probably not that different from many of us (even if you don't go jogging) – she's a hard worker, trying her best to carry on, make ends meet and continue living her life. We meet the Jogger as she is feeling the weight of living in a world impacted by COVID-19 – and she is struggling.

She is someone who, in her best moments, manages to cope but, in her worst, nearly gives up. Our Jogger is not a hero. Nor is she trying to lecture or preach to you. We believe that people don't like to be told what to do, but every person has the potential to inspire others – in unique, unexpected and diverse ways. As well as following the Jogger's narrative, this book contains examples and activities for you to try out – for yourself or with somebody else. The activities are an invitation for you to take it or leave it, just as the Jogger does – sometimes intrigued, sometimes suspicious, sometimes curious.

As is the nature of all conversations, we listen and respond to what has been said. While seeing the conversations unfold throughout this book, it is worth paying particular attention to the questions being asked and the responses to them. You will also have the opportunity to try out and experience these questions for yourself at the end of each chapter. It is through these questions that we try to be as useful as we can to others and ourselves.

And as the story progresses, you'll see, and hopefully experience for yourself, the impact these simple questions can have in helping to improve lives. Despite the continuous change and uncertainties we face as a result of COVID-19, these conversations remain useful, giving us hope, reminding us what we're capable of, and inspiring us to carry on the best way we can.

ONE

IT'S TOO MUCH

'Life has a way of breaking even
the strongest among us.'
Sherrilyn Kenyon

It was a Saturday morning. One of those days when
the Jogger hoped to sleep in a little longer to escape
the chaos and uncertainty in her life, even if just for
a few minutes. The children woke early and were
bursting with the kind of energy that only young kids
have at six in the morning. Thankfully, the Jogger's
partner went downstairs with the children to make
breakfast, though she knew they would expect her to
join them shortly.

While lying in bed, she felt the tension in her jaw
as her heart rate accelerated. It didn't take long before
all the thoughts that had been plaguing her flooded
back in.

How did we get to this point?
Am I having another panic attack?
Are we going to have enough money this month?

The Jogger turned to grab her phone and check her
bank balance, a habit she'd picked up since the first
lockdown. As a family, they could maybe just make

it with the money they had left. After closing that down, her news app alerted her to even more changes around COVID-19 restrictions – something about only meeting with a certain number of people, whether or not you could go to restaurants, and the necessity of wearing a face mask while on public transport.

Trying not to get too caught up in it all, the Jogger sluggishly got up and sat on the edge of the bed. Looking in a mirror, she noticed the few extra pounds she'd put on during the most recent lockdown, despite her best efforts to stay active. She thought about all the chocolate and ice cream she'd been eating more frequently – and the extra drinks. She knew all these things weren't helpful, but food and alcohol had sometimes been a great comfort over these past months.

Still in her pyjamas, the Jogger heard the noise coming from the front room. She knew, without having to go downstairs, that her three children were watching one of the online exercise videos, which were supposed to be a replacement for PE lessons in school. The thudding of feet echoed up the stairs, accompanied by the instructor's exuberant voice.

As the volume in the front room continued to rise, she heard her seven-year-old son half-singing, half-shouting along with the music and her five-year-old daughter laughing. Knowing that when her children spent this much time together in an enclosed space disaster would soon follow, she anticipated an argument within seconds.

And right on cue, the laughter and singing turned to bickering, followed by the thud of something or someone hitting the floor. The Jogger's heart started to race as she realised she hadn't heard anything from her two-year-old son. She flew down the stairs, almost tripping head first as she braced herself for what had happened in the front room.

With her adrenaline surging, the Jogger turned the corner into the front room and thankfully found her partner calming things down.

THE JOGGER: What happened?
THE PARTNER: Oh nothing, they were just playing with the cushions on the sofa and falling to the floor when they hit each other.
THE JOGGER: How many times do I have to tell you guys to be careful in here?
THE PARTNER: It's all right. They're just playing.

From the tone of her partner's voice, the Jogger knew that this conversation would not end well for any of them if it continued.

THE JOGGER: Fine. I'm going to make breakfast.

The only sound the Jogger heard as she stomped towards the kitchen was the PE instructor's gleeful voice:

'Good work! Let's keep going!'

These videos had been so beneficial for the whole family, but right now that gleeful voice was beginning to grate. As she stood in the kitchen with her hands on the countertop, head held low, memories started to rush in of the times when she hadn't handled things very well – they usually ended with the kids in tears and an argument with her partner. This was not how the Jogger wanted to be as a parent. This was not the example she wanted to set for her children.

Tears started to well. Not wanting anyone in the family to see her like this, she quickly rubbed her eyes, put some cereal into a bowl and poured a glass of orange juice. As she walked over to sit down and eat, she was confronted with the dining table. It was too small for the family of five, and was covered in various books, worksheets and random pages of colouring-in from the schoolwork that she and her partner had tried to help the kids with during the week.

As the Jogger thought back to yesterday, all she could think about was the disaster that had taken place while she was simply trying to support her eldest with his reading, teach her daughter some phonics and entertain her youngest with a bit of drawing. It all started well enough, but it quickly turned into chaos as the children shouted at each other, threw things across the table and then refused to do any work. The Jogger's own frustration was difficult to manage, let alone the frustration of her three kids.

Wincing at the memory, she put her breakfast down on the kitchen countertop so she could deal with the debris on the table. Shoving everything into one pile, she carelessly dumped it onto one of the dining chairs.

With the table now cleared, she had space to eat her breakfast in peace. However, shortly after she sat down, a creaking door announced the entrance of her partner. With her mouth full of cereal, the Jogger spluttered and frantically waved as he pulled out the chair covered in books and worksheets. Tumbling onto the floor, the avalanche of paper scattered everywhere.

THE PARTNER: Seriously?

THE JOGGER: Just leave it. I'll get it in a minute.

THE PARTNER: What was all of that doing on the chair? It was on the table when I was in here a minute ago.

THE JOGGER: Yeah, well, I moved it.

THE PARTNER: Why didn't you put it all away?

THE JOGGER: Because I just wanted to eat my breakfast, and I was tired of looking at it. It was the last thing I wanted to see right now, especially as it's Saturday.

THE PARTNER: Next time, can't you just put everything away? You know I'm trying to keep all their stuff in their own folders.

THE JOGGER: Yeah, sure. Whatever.

Facing another example of something she'd got wrong, the Jogger let out a heavy sigh as she trudged around the table, bent down and picked everything up off the floor.

THE JOGGER: There. Are you happy now?

THE PARTNER: What is *wrong* with you?

THE JOGGER: Nothing. I'm fine.

THE PARTNER: Yeah. Sure. And pigs can fly. You looked like you were about to bite the kids' heads off when you came downstairs, and now you're sulking like a child.

THE JOGGER: Wow. Thanks.

THE PARTNER: You're welcome.

THE JOGGER: Look, it's been a long week for me, and I'm struggling a bit.

Her partner's eyebrows shot up in shock.

THE PARTNER: It's been a long week for *you*? I've been doing most of the work around here. I'm pretty sure I've been waking up with the kids and doing everything in the mornings for a while now while you've been sleeping in.

THE JOGGER: You've got to be kidding me. I've been helping them with all their homework, getting their lunches ready, and making sure they get to bed on time. You just get to do the fun bits and play with the kids. It must be easy for you to be the fun parent, but one of us has to do the hard work.

Her partner threw his hands up in despair.

THE PARTNER: It's hopeless talking to you when you're like this. Just go. Go for a run or something.

7

THE JOGGER: That's the first good idea you've had for months. I think I'll do just that. I'll be gone for a while – just so you can see what it's like to look after the three of them for a full day on your own.

With that, the Jogger furiously made her way upstairs to get changed. She slammed the bedroom door, and the sound of it echoed through the entire house.

TWO

EVERYTHING STARTS WITH HOPE

'Hope is being able to see that
there is light despite all of the
darkness.'

Desmond Tutu

The Jogger sighed as she bent down to tie the laces
of her scuffed running shoes. As she reached for
her keys, she fumbled and dropped them. The front
door was so heavy and the handle so stiff that she
welcomed the opportunity to give the door a bit
of a kick. Stepping onto the porch, she realised her
keys were still on the doormat. With reluctance, she
turned back to pick them up.

In the midst of all the stress and worry, the
arguments and panic attacks, there was one thing
the Jogger found to be a little helpful, and that was
going for a run. These runs were in part a desperate
attempt to clear her head – and if ever there was a day
when she needed to clear her head it was today. She
hadn't meant to snap and lose her temper earlier, but
the mounting difficulties and ear-splitting noise of
the household had become too much.

Standing on the pathway outside her house as she

put on her face mask, the Jogger felt a cold breeze drift over her skin. Hazy sunlight beckoned through the overcast sky. 'Yes,' she thought to herself, 'this is what I need.' She turned to find her elderly neighbour Bill examining his car. Prior to COVID-19, he would often have greeted her with a hug, but these days he took social distancing seriously. Regardless of the few metres between them, Bill's smile was as warm and welcoming as ever.

Bill was known to everyone as a lovable but quirky man. His wife had sadly passed away a few years ago, and since then his passion had been a vintage classic car, which was parked on the road, wheels almost kissing the kerb. The pristine grey 1964 Austin Cambridge was a four-door saloon with a deep red interior.

Bill was devoted to that car, washing and polishing it every weekend until it was so sparkling the Jogger felt as if she needed sunglasses to look at it.

Although she knew a great deal about Bill's car,

she had to admit she didn't know that much about the man himself. He would talk for hours if you let him, so much so that the Jogger would often find herself daydreaming as he rambled on. Today that daydreaming was dedicated to the turbulence of her home life and the argument with her partner.

BILL: Morning! How are you today?
THE JOGGER: Morning, Bill. I'm all right, thanks. And yourself?

In truth, the Jogger didn't feel all right, nor did she have the energy to listen to Bill's rambling, but she hoped a few pleasantries would end the conversation quickly. But Bill, it seemed, neither knew nor cared to follow the rules of small talk.

BILL: Fantastic! Where are you off to today?
THE JOGGER: Just out for a run ... I, umm ...

The Jogger struggled for a way out of the conversation, while Bill maintained a patient and steady gaze. There was no getting out of this without seeming rude, so she smiled and continued with another question.

THE JOGGER: What are you up to, Bill?

Anticipating the question, he sidestepped gracefully to allow the Jogger full view of the Austin Cambridge.

BILL: I've been taking care of this beauty! What
do you think?

The old man spread his arms like a proud ring-
master, inviting his audience of one to survey the
pristine motor.

THE JOGGER: Wow! You've done a great job.
BILL: Thank you. She's my treasure, this car is.

A few rays of sunlight slipped through the clouds and
danced on the car's spotless surface. The more the
Jogger looked at it, the more impressed she was.

THE JOGGER: So, what's she like to drive?
BILL: I wouldn't know nowadays.

A grin crept across Bill's face as he continued to
carefully polish the already immaculate bodywork,
determined not to leave a single scuff.

THE JOGGER: What do you mean you wouldn't
know?
BILL: Well, I can't drive anymore – they said my
eyesight's not up to it.
THE JOGGER: Then why ... I don't get ...
BILL: [laughing] What don't you get?
THE JOGGER: I mean, why would you spend so
much time and effort washing and polishing a
car that you can't drive anymore?

The thought of painstakingly caring for a car you couldn't even drive seemed absurd to the Jogger. Surely the old man wouldn't be able to talk himself out of this one. Sensing a hint of confusion creeping over Bill's face, the Jogger was surprised when his expression turned into a mischievous smile.

BILL: Aha! That's easy to answer.

THE JOGGER: Really?

BILL: Of course! My hope from washing and polishing the car has nothing to do with driving it.

A glint flashed across his eyes as if he'd just played his best poker hand.

THE JOGGER: I don't quite understand.

BILL: You see, I believe that many good things start with one's hopes. So my hope from keeping the car sparkling isn't about driving it – it's that every now and then someone will see it and appreciate it. My hope is to bring a smile to people's faces, so I polish the car … and sometimes it works … you're smiling now!

THE JOGGER: That's true, you have made me smile. But I still don't get it. Surely you're not out here every weekend, working this hard, just to make the occasional person smile?

BILL: Well, I have to admit that it makes a difference to me too. Making other people smile was something my wife did her best to do wherever she went. After she died, working on the car and seeing other people appreciate and enjoy it has given me a renewed sense of purpose. So I suppose you could say that my hopes are to make other people happy, to give me purpose and to honour my wife. So you see, it's my hopes that inspire my actions.

The Jogger was taken aback. She'd seen Bill polishing his car weekend after weekend, but was only now discovering why.

THE JOGGER: I knew the car meant a lot to you, but I had no idea you were doing it for your wife.

BILL: She was always trying to brighten someone's day, so this is one way I can continue to do that now that she's gone.

THE JOGGER: I can see now how your hopes inspire you to do what you do.

BILL: Of course, it's the same for all of us – our hopes inspire our actions.

There was something about Bill's words that resonated with her.

Taking out her phone, the Jogger opened up her notes, scrolling past countless old shopping lists before typing what Bill had said:

our hopes inspire our actions

THE JOGGER: So, you're saying the reason
   you're out here every weekend is all down to
   your various hopes?
BILL: Absolutely. If my hope had been to
   maintain the car so that I could drive it, I
   might well have become frustrated and given
   up. Keeping it pristine in the hope of making
   other people smile, finding a greater sense of
   purpose and honouring my wife … now that's
   a different matter entirely.
THE JOGGER: I see …

The Jogger was surprised to find that the silence
that had settled over the conversation was more
contemplative than awkward.

BILL: So, what about you? What is it that you're
   hoping for from your run today?
THE JOGGER: What? My run? I don't know …
   I'm just running … well, trying to anyway. I'm
   not really hoping for anything from it.

To her surprise, Bill rattled out a disbelieving laugh.
Not that it was a mean laugh; there was a glimmer of
kindness in his eyes that never seemed to leave him.

BILL: Of course you're hoping for something
   from your run, otherwise you wouldn't go! So
   what is it?

How had the Jogger managed to get into this situation? She'd only meant to have a brief chat, and yet here she was, answering question after question. Checking her watch and seeing only ten minutes had passed since the conversation began, she decided she might as well entertain Bill's quizzing a little longer.

THE JOGGER: I suppose I'm hoping I might get rid of some of the stress and panic churning in my brain at the moment.

BILL: I see. And if the stress and panic dissipate as you run, what would you be hoping to find instead?

THE JOGGER: I really don't know ... I just can't see how anything will help at the moment. There's so much uncertainty around COVID and so many things to worry about.

BILL: It is a difficult time, that's for sure, and a lot of things are out of our control. Suppose this run does help ease some of that stress and panic, what are you hoping will replace them?

THE JOGGER: Just being able to clear my mind would be a help, and to start thinking straight again.

BILL: And if you had a clearer mind and were thinking straight, what difference do you think that would make?

THE JOGGER: Erm ... I guess I might be more relaxed, and perhaps move forward with my life a little.

BILL: Aha! There it is!

THE JOGGER: There is what?

BILL: Your hope!

THE JOGGER: My hope?

BILL: Yes, your hope that has inspired or maybe even pushed you to go out running today, hoping to relax and move forward with your life. But that's just my guess and I might be rambling again. Don't take an old man like me too seriously.

The Jogger was once again taken by surprise. If she was being honest, that was indeed what she'd been hoping for, though she'd never thought about it like that – she'd never thought about her actions being driven by her hope.

THE JOGGER: Well ... yes ... I guess so. And you're not rambling at all, Bill.

Just as Bill was folding in the outside wing mirror of the Austin, a speeding, battered Peugeot came roaring around the corner. If the Jogger had been standing in the road right now, she might have been inclined to jump back. But Bill didn't seem too flustered. With a wry smile, he took a small step backwards, allowing the Peugeot to pass – missing his toes by only a few millimetres. Sliding into the free spot between Bill's car and another neighbour's, the Peugeot came to a smooth stop. The Jogger had never seen parallel parking executed so perfectly.

BILL: That's Katya, our dear girl. Have you met
    her before? She lives further down in flat 18
    and is quite a powerhouse!

The Jogger knew a little about Katya. She was a
local girl renowned for her artistic abilities. Not
too long ago, she had created a beautiful painting of
wildflowers. Just looking at it, the Jogger could see
the hundreds of hours Katya had devoted to her craft
– the delicate brushstrokes, the lifelike imagery. It
had been displayed in the community hall, a tribute
to her talent and the pride of the neighbourhood. But
Katya had since taken the painting down, apparently
ashamed of its flaws – flaws only she could see.

As Katya wrestled with the shopping bags in the
boot of her car, Bill took the opportunity to tell the
Jogger a little more about her.

BILL: When Katya stopped by the other week,
    I could tell that, like you, she was in need of
    some hope.

Katya planted her shopping bags on the path and
pushed her glasses higher up the bridge of her nose,
taking care not to dislodge her colourful mask. Her
baggy sleeves partly hid splotches of paint on her
agile hands.

KATYA: Hi, Bill!

Katya's muscles seemed to twitch, ready to reach
for a hug, then she stepped back, remembering the
COVID-19 distancing.

BILL: Hi, Katya, great to see you. This is my
neighbour.

A beaming smile greeted the Jogger, who returned
the acknowledgement. This courteous person with
a delicate frame was not the driver she had imagined
after witnessing the Peugeot career around the corner
only moments earlier.

THE JOGGER: Nice to meet you.
KATYA: Likewise.
BILL: I was just about to tell her about our
interesting conversation on finding hope. And
voila – you blew in like a tornado!

Katya clicked her key fob to make sure the car was
locked. Pocketing the keys, she leaned against a
nearby lamp post.

KATYA: I remember every word of that
conversation. I was having such a rough day
and our chat and those questions you asked
were really helpful.
BILL: Do you remember how I asked you about
what your hopes were?
KATYA: I do. Let's see ... I think I said I wanted
to get back to a positive mindset, because I'd
been struggling to see the good in anything
that week.
BILL: That's right ...

He looked over at the Jogger, checking that she was following the details.

BILL: ... and I asked what difference getting back to a positive mindset would make to you.

Katya lifted her head towards the sky.

KATYA: I remember that question really making me think about how I'd enjoy life more and do better with my painting and my career.

A pigeon fluttered past, causing the Jogger to jump and lose concentration for a moment.

THE JOGGER: Sorry, what was that question again? The one that really made you think?
BILL: It was a rather simple one. Katya said she'd like to get back to her positive mindset, so I asked her what difference it would make to have that. In fact, I think I used a similar question after that, asking what difference it would make if she was enjoying life more and doing better with her painting.

Recalling the conversation further, Katya began waving her hand as if painting a canvas.

KATYA: That question made me think I'd probably be making more of an effort with my friends, even though it's hard to see them in person at the moment.

THE JOGGER: So after just a few short questions you'd already listed all those things?

A grin crept across Katya's face, her eyes bright with possibility.

KATYA: Yes, all those things, and that wasn't even all of it. Bill asked me what else I'd like to add to that list.

THE JOGGER: [laughing] What did you tell him?

The Jogger cut her laughter short as she noticed Katya's brow furrow slightly and her gaze drift down to her feet.

KATYA: Actually, I told him about some difficult stuff at that point. About how I sometimes get overwhelmed with self-doubt. How I have loads of things I want to achieve, but the self-doubt sometimes stops me from pursuing them.

The Jogger looked towards Bill. This appeared to be the first part of the recounted conversation that hadn't gone smoothly. Running his fingers through his thinning silver hair, Bill watched and listened patiently as Katya continued.

KATYA: Like the time there was this gallery exhibition competition. I thought I would give it a try. I even started coming up with ideas. But then I thought, 'No, I'm not good enough.' Which was stupid.

Bill remained silent, so the Jogger tentatively asked another question.

THE JOGGER: So how did Bill respond when you told him about your struggles with self-doubt?

Laughing spontaneously, Katya shook her head in amusement.

KATYA: It was ridiculously simple, really. He just asked me what I wanted to be happening instead.
THE JOGGER: I see. And what did you want instead?
KATYA: I told him I wanted to be giving things a go.

Finally, Bill interjected.

BILL: And when you said you wanted to be giving things a go, I also asked what you thought that might lead to. Especially if you were doing so with a positive mindset.
KATYA: You did, yes, and that's when I said I'd

feel better about myself and would start to
have more of a life plan.

THE JOGGER: So by the end of this chat you'd
named a whole bunch of hopes?

KATYA: Yup. To reinforce a positive mindset,
enjoy life more, do better with my painting,
be excited about the future, make an effort
with friends, give things a go, and have more
of a life plan.

Bill and Katya exchanged a grin. No longer looking at
her feet, she was again bright and animated.

KATYA: So that's how the conversation about
my hopes went. And by the end, I knew that
if I could see progress in those things, then I'd
be heading in a good direction. It was a really
helpful discussion, though Bill refuses to take
any credit!

BILL: Of course not. The ideas were all yours – I
just asked about them.

Katya's mobile phone rang.

KATYA: Sorry, I'll have to take this, it's a friend.
Good to see you both!

THE JOGGER: And you. I should probably get
going anyway. Thanks so much to both of you
for your time, it's been ... interesting.

Bill started to rummage around in his overall pockets.

Pulling out a scrap of coffee-stained paper, he presented it to the Jogger.

BILL: Here, before you go, take this. It's a little task I gave Katya. Think of it as 'an invitation for discovering hopes'.

Taking the crumpled piece of paper, the Jogger unfolded it to reveal the following questions:

HOPES

What are your best hopes right now?

If those hopes were achieved, what difference would they make?

What difference would those differences make?

If those hopes and differences were achieved, what might they lead to?

The Jogger took a snapshot of the crumpled piece of paper, careful to include the whole page, and saved it on her phone, alongside the note she'd made earlier. Thanking Bill again and turning to continue on her way, the Jogger couldn't help but dwell on that phrase: our hopes inspire our actions.

Activity/Exercise

Thinking of Bill's questions, try answering them yourself:

> What are your best hopes at this point in time?

> If these hopes were achieved, what difference would they make?

> What difference would those differences make?

> If these hopes and differences were achieved, what might they lead to?

THREE

THE IMAGE OF A FUTURE WORTH LIVING

'The future belongs to those
who believe in the beauty of
their dreams.'

Eleanor Roosevelt

The Jogger's mind was racing with new thoughts after her conversation with Bill. What he'd said resonated with her in a promising way, but his approach to life still wasn't entirely adding up. It was all very well to say that 'our hopes inspire our actions,' but what then?

Panting heavily, the Jogger wound her way through the neighbourhood's streets of semi-detached houses. Turning the corner towards a nearby park, she almost knocked into a woman walking her dog. The feisty Yorkshire terrier fixed its eyes on the Jogger and gave a not so intimidating growl. The dog walker gasped behind her face mask, visibly shaken.

THE JOGGER: I'm really sorry! Are you OK?
THE DOG WALKER: I'm fine, I'm fine, but you
  need to look where you're going and stop
  staring at your feet!
THE JOGGER: I know, I'm so sorry, it's just that
  I was …

As the dog walker regained her poise and adjusted
her spectacles, she noticed the Jogger's furrowed
brow.

THE DOG WALKER: Something the matter,
  dear?
THE JOGGER: No … nothing much.

THE DOG WALKER: Come on, I've seen expressions like that before. What's bothering you?

The woman was persistent, and it seemed unlikely the Jogger could get away with shrugging off the well-intended question. Besides, she owed an action of apology, so the least she could do was answer her, even if the Yorkshire terrier was now growling like a lawn mower.

THE JOGGER: It's just something my neighbour said to me.
THE DOG WALKER: And what was that?

As a cyclist whizzed past and another dog walker crossed the road to avoid the growling terrier, the Jogger took a moment to glance purposefully at her watch. She hadn't anticipated one conversation interrupting her run, let alone two.

THE DOG WALKER: Don't worry, dear, I've lots of time on my hands. Please go on.
THE JOGGER: I don't really … I'm not … My neighbour asked a lot of questions about hope, and I ended up saying that my hope was to move forward with my life.
THE DOG WALKER: And is that true?
THE JOGGER: Yeah, I guess so.
THE DOG WALKER: Then what's troubling you?
THE JOGGER: I just don't know how I'm

supposed to do that. I mean, I don't know *how*
I'm going to move forward with my life. Right
now, all I have is hope.

A perceptive look passed over the dog walker's face.
Even the little dog yapped and looked up at his owner
as if he was in on the secret.

THE DOG WALKER: Ah – you're stuck on the
'how do I get there?' question. That one's
stumped me many times over the years.
THE JOGGER: Huh? How do you mean?
THE DOG WALKER: It seems the obvious thing
to ask, doesn't it? How do I do this? How do I
get there? But obvious questions aren't always
the most helpful or useful ones.

This was turning into a strange day. The Jogger was
reluctant to get dragged into another conversation,
however warm and motherly this woman seemed.
On the other hand, the conversation with Bill had
been surprisingly helpful. Maybe this one would be
too.

THE JOGGER: I agree that asking myself how
I'm going to get there hasn't been particularly
helpful so far, but what do you think would be
a better question?
THE DOG WALKER: This might sound funny
but my dog, Einstein, taught me the answer to
that one.

She then picked up Einstein, who proceeded to lick her neck and wag his tail. An absolute charmer now, it appeared.

THE DOG WALKER: You see, one of Einstein's favourite things in the world is food.
THE JOGGER: I could have guessed that. But I don't quite see how that helps me.
THE DOG WALKER: Let me ask you this ... Do you think Einstein wastes much time thinking about how he's going to get his food?
THE JOGGER: I've no idea – he's a dog!
THE DOG WALKER: I know him rather well, and I reckon he spends more time thinking about what it's going to taste like than where it's going to come from.

The Jogger glanced at the little dog, who was licking his lips after hearing the word 'food'.

THE JOGGER: I can believe that!
THE DOG WALKER: [laughing] A while ago, I tried to adopt the same thinking.
THE JOGGER: And how did that work out?
THE DOG WALKER: It worked out really well. It turns out it's much more helpful to think about what your life will be like once your hopes have been achieved, rather than what you need to do to achieve them. You focus on what your life will look like, as opposed to how to get there.

THE JOGGER: Hmm ... I'm still not sure I get it.

The dog walker adjusted her glasses again. Einstein settled himself against her shoulder, shuffling until he was comfortable. There was no social distancing applied to dogs, and it appeared he knew this conversation needed some room to grow.

THE DOG WALKER: OK, let's put it another way. Why did you almost crash into me a minute ago?

THE JOGGER: Because I wasn't looking where I was going? And again, I'm so sorry.

THE DOG WALKER: It's all right, I'm fine. Back to my question though, where were you looking instead?

THE JOGGER: Well, down at my feet ...

The dog walker clicked her fingers in triumph.

THE DOG WALKER: Precisely! You were too caught up in looking at your current steps.

THE JOGGER: Huh?

THE DOG WALKER: You were so focused on the steps you were taking that you forgot to look up, to look ahead to where you were going.

THE JOGGER: Right, but I'm still not following. How on earth does that relate to your little dog and his food? And how does it relate to my situation?

THE DOG WALKER: I mean that Einstein

doesn't get too caught up on the steps he
needs to take to get his food. He focuses more
on looking ahead to what it will taste like.

THE JOGGER: So you're saying I should stop
worrying so much about what steps I need to
take, and start looking ahead to where I want
to be as if I were already there?

THE DOG WALKER: Exactly. If all you're doing
is focusing on what steps you need to take,
then you might end up missing the signs that
you're heading in the right direction.

THE JOGGER: OK, I think that makes sense. I
need to start thinking about signs rather than
steps? About what I want my future to be
like, rather than how to get there or what's
stopping me?

THE DOG WALKER: Yes, that's right – you've
got it. Now let's take your situation as an
example.

The Jogger was starting to feel enthusiastic; it seemed
there was something useful in what the dog walker
was saying after all.

THE DOG WALKER: So rather than getting
stuck trying to figure out what steps you need
to take to move forward with your life, let me
ask you this instead – what will be the first
sign that you're moving forward with your
life?

The Jogger paused. She'd been asked questions about 'moving forward' before, but usually it was around *how* she would move forward, what she needed to do, what steps she needed to take and what obstacles were in the way. She couldn't remember a time when she'd been asked to consider the *signs* that she was moving forward.

THE JOGGER: Hmm, I suppose I might start to enjoy my runs a little more, rather than just using them to vent stress.

THE DOG WALKER: Great. And how would you know you were enjoying your runs a little more?

THE JOGGER: Maybe I'd start to notice more of the things around me, more of the sights and smells and sounds … and people.

THE DOG WALKER: Indeed. And what sorts of sights and smells and sounds would that be?

THE JOGGER: Maybe the clouds, the aroma from the coffee shop, the rustle of the leaves. All those things I'm usually too stressed to notice.

THE DOG WALKER: And on this occasion, when you *do* notice those things, what difference will that make?

The Jogger had heard that question before! It was just like one Bill had asked earlier, when she first set out on her run.

THE JOGGER: What difference ... maybe
noticing those things might clear my head a
bit, I guess. I might start to feel a little better
about the world.

THE DOG WALKER: Excellent. Is it OK to ask a
few more questions?

THE JOGGER: Sure, carry on.

By this point she was enthusiastic about the prospect
of further questions from the dog walker. Thoughts
of the difficulties triggered by COVID-19 were being
replaced by more hopeful future ones – not just about
the rest of her run, but also the rest of her day.

THE DOG WALKER: If you were enjoying your
run a bit more, noticing more of the things
around you, did you say you might start to feel
a little better about the world?

THE JOGGER: Yeah, I guess so.

THE DOG WALKER: And how will this feeling a
little better about the world show in what you
do next?

THE JOGGER: I'm not sure.

THE DOG WALKER: Mmmm. That's OK, it's a
strange question. How do you think feeling
a little better about the world might show in
what you do next?

THE JOGGER: I guess I'd probably be able to
engage more with the world than I have been.

The clouds shifted, their shadows dancing with each

other on the pavement, rather like the dog walker's questions were dancing with the Jogger's answers.

THE DOG WALKER: Engaging more with the world? What do you imagine that will look like?
THE JOGGER: I think being more open, talking to more people, reaching out to friends I haven't spoken to in ages. Being more present with my family.
THE DOG WALKER: And out of all those people you mentioned, who do you think will notice you engaging with the world most?
THE JOGGER: Probably my kids.

Nodding to herself, the Jogger smiled at the thought of her children noticing this change in her. As if on cue, jubilant giggling from children in a nearby garden spilled out onto the street.

THE DOG WALKER: So what will be a sign to your kids that you're engaging more with the world, feeling a bit better about it while doing so, and being more present with them?
THE JOGGER: Maybe the way I greet them when I get home.
THE DOG WALKER: How will you be greeting them that shows you're feeling better about the world and engaging with it? And sorry if I'm being too curious!
THE JOGGER: No worries, it's interesting to

think like this. I'd greet them with a big hug
and a smile on my face.

THE DOG WALKER: Lovely, greeting them with
a smile and a hug. And how do you think will
they respond to that?

THE JOGGER: [laughing] They'll probably get
excited and give me a big hug back.

The Jogger felt a pleasant shiver of emotion run up
her spine as she thought about her family. Surely it
couldn't be this simple: just think about where you
want to be, not how to get there. It still seemed too
easy.

THE JOGGER: OK, I'll admit you've got some
clever questions but, come on, isn't it just a
trick?

A wry grin spread across the Jogger's face.

THE DOG WALKER: [laughing] I wouldn't
consider them clever questions – in fact,
I like to think they're rather simple. The
challenge is in persisting and sticking with
them until you find the answers. And no, it's
not some magical trick – it really works. I've
seen evidence of it over and over with lots of
different people ... and I've been around for a
very long time.

THE JOGGER: In what way does it work?

THE DOG WALKER: Well, having spoken and

thought about what it would be like, would
you say the possibility of you greeting your
kids with a hug and smile has increased or
decreased?

The Jogger paused to consider. She was genuinely
looking forward to greeting her kids with a big hug
now.

THE JOGGER: Increased, definitely.

THE DOG WALKER: OK. And thinking back to
my Einstein with his food, do you think he's
more or less likely to find a way of persuading
me to feed him if he's spent an hour thinking
of how delicious it will be?

THE JOGGER: [laughing] More likely, I would
think.

The dog walker nodded in encouragement. Einstein
licked his lips and drooled a little.

THE DOG WALKER: As simple as that. If you
keep your eyes focused on where you want to
go and what it will be like, then your feet, and
steps, will naturally follow.

'Gran! Graaaan!' The sound of quickening steps
accompanied the voice of a young boy who whisked
around the corner and jumped to a halt, saluting like
a soldier. Two lines of mud were streaked across each
of his cheeks and a sword-like stick was tucked under

one arm.

THE DOG WALKER: Aiden! How lovely to
see you, and perfect timing too! Could you
explain to our friend here a bit about that
project you and your friends have been
working on in the woods?
AIDEN: You mean our secret hideout? Sure!

The Jogger glanced down at her watch once more.
Time was really ticking on. However, the boy's
enthusiasm to tell his story was inescapable. The way
Aiden's feet started to dance on the pavement with
excitement as he began to speak reminded her of her
eldest son.

AIDEN: So, me and my friends wanted to build a
super-cool hideout!
THE JOGGER: That sounds exciting!
AIDEN: Yeah, it was – but we didn't really know
how to start. Our first one collapsed … That's
when my gran helped us.
THE JOGGER: [laughing] Let me guess – she
asked you a load of questions?
AIDEN: Yup – that's what my gran does best.
Oh, and baking cakes!
THE JOGGER: So what did she ask you?

He pondered for a moment, evoking the memory of
his gran's wise words.

AIDEN: I think it went like this ...

Scratching his head and squinting with concentration, Aiden meticulously recounted the historical conversation with his grandmother, starting with a pretty good impression of her voice:

GRAN: There's no need to get upset, Aiden. I know building your hideout seems really difficult, but just for a moment, don't worry about how you're going to build it. Tell me instead a bit about what you hope it's going to be like. What are some of your ideas?

AIDEN: We want it to be the best hideout ever!

GRAN: I see. So how will you know that it's the best hideout ever?

AIDEN: It will have a flag on the top – a red one. There will be enough room for all five of us to hide inside, and it'll have lookouts high up off the ground, with bridges in between, and a rope swing!

GRAN: Sounds marvellous! What else will you notice about it that shows it's the best hideout ever?

AIDEN: Erm ... It'll have hammocks, ladders, a slide and windows to shoot arrows out of. There'll be a gap in the roof, so we can see the stars, and a secret trap door. Oh, and it'll be camouflaged too!

GRAN: Wow! And how do you think your friends are going to react when you've all finished building it?

AIDEN: They're gonna go crazy! They'll love it!

GRAN: How will you know that they love it?

AIDEN: We'll be the kings of the castle, and they'll never want to leave! Not even when their mums come to get them! It'll be awesome!

GRAN: And how will you react to your friends being the kings of the castle with you, and not wanting to leave because they love it so much?

AIDEN: I'll be super excited too. It'll be the best place ever!

GRAN: And when you're standing there, looking at your finished hideout, what will be the thing that pleases you the most about it?

AIDEN: Everything!

GRAN: Well, Aiden, it sounds like the possibilities are endless! I look forward to seeing it when you're finished.

Beaming, the young boy looked up at the Jogger to signal his anecdote had reached its end.

AIDEN: So, what do you think?

THE JOGGER: That's certainly a very interesting story, Aiden, and the hideout sounds brilliant, but what happened to it? Did it ever get built?

AIDEN: You bet! I mean, it's a bit different to how we imagined. It's not quite the same shape and the flag blew down ... But it's still awesome!

THE JOGGER: You figured out how to build it after all?

AIDEN: Yup – my gran was right, as usual.

He glanced up at his gran, who gave him a proud grin.

AIDEN: Once we'd dreamed about what the hideout would look like, the rest was easy! We were so excited to get started that we didn't even have to think much about how to build it. We just sort of worked it out as we went along. Turned out we were already great at building hideouts.

The boy unzipped his bag and pulled out a detailed drawing of the hideout.

AIDEN: Here, this is an activity my gran gave
me to help us on our way. Since the hideout
is finished now, I don't need it anymore – but
maybe you want it?
THE JOGGER: Oh, yes please! Thank you!

The Jogger surveyed the magnificent drawing, noting
the words proudly displayed at the top of the image:
Aiden's 'Home of Possibilities'. Below the illustration
was a list of questions, presumably from his gran.

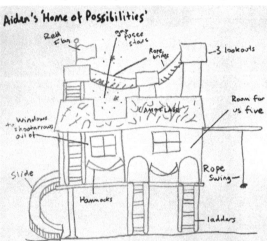

What will be the first sign that your hopes have come true?
What else will tell you that what you're hoping for
has been achieved?
What will you notice about yourself
that shows your hopes are present?
What will others notice?   How will they react?
How will you respond to their reaction?
What difference will that make?
Having achieved your hopes, what will please you most?

As the Jogger said her goodbyes, thanking the dog walker, her grandson and Einstein, she thought about what she had just heard. From now on, she decided, she would look ahead instead of down at her feet all the time. She would try to shift her attention more towards what she hoped her future would be like, rather than how to get there.

Thinking more about what she hoped her future would be like, the Jogger's thoughts returned to her family. She couldn't leave things the way they were. Pulling out her phone, she continued towards a nearby park and thought about the text message she was about to send her partner.

Activity/Exercise:

If you would find it helpful, perhaps take a moment to answer the dog walker's questions for yourself:

> What will be the first sign that your hopes have come true?
>
> What else will tell you that what you're hoping for has been achieved?
>
> What will you notice about yourself that shows your hopes are present?
>
> What will others notice?
>
> How will they react?

How will you respond to their reaction?

What difference will that make?

Having achieved your hopes, what will please you most?

FOUR

Overcoming Challenge

> 'Sometimes what you want is
> right in front of you. All you
> have to do is open your eyes
> and see it.'
>
> *Meg Cabot*

As the Jogger continued her run, she was unsure what message to send. Thinking back to her previous conversation, she focused on her hopes and how she wanted things to be.

THE JOGGER: [texting] I'm sorry. I don't want things to be like that between us. It's hard enough as it is, even with the two of us working together. I want things to be better for us, for our family, like they used to be.

Feeling unsure of what the response would be and where things might go for them as a couple, the Jogger was left with a sense of anxiety, but also a sense of hope as she continued to think about the wealth of possibilities that might lie ahead. She realised she'd been only half-concentrating on where she was going until now. With the number of people out in the park today, and having already almost knocked the dog walker over, she decided it was best to find a place to sit down so she could try to make sense of her thoughts.

She sat down on the nearest bench, almost bumping into the current occupant.

Quickly apologising, she jumped up as the woman took an apple and two bananas from her bag while talking to her children – two girls and a boy. They were older than the Jogger's children. The mother, clearly not making any headway, addressed the Jogger.

THE MOTHER: At least somebody is interested in this fruit. Give me a chance to sort out their snack, and I'll see what we have left for you.

THE JOGGER: Oh, don't worry about me, I'm
    not picky when it comes to food.

The woman returned to the conversation with her
children. Feeling as though she was intruding, the
Jogger moved to the next bench along. The mother
tried to coax her children into eating the fruit.
Predictably, they took the chocolate from her bag
instead, then they ran off to play. Having now sorted
out the snack, and with the children's scooters strewn
around the bench, the mother looked over at the
Jogger.

THE MOTHER: Well, they're not going to eat
    any of this. What about you? Would you like
    a banana or an apple?

She reached over, offering a small bottle of hand
sanitiser to the Jogger, who was sitting on her own
bench, hunched over with her forearms on her
thighs. Still clutching her phone and hoping for a
response from her partner, she was staring into the
distance and didn't hear what the woman had said to
her.

THE MOTHER: Are you OK? You look like
    you're really thinking about something.
THE JOGGER: Yeah, just having one of those
    days where I'm miles away.

Still feeling a bit out of sorts and wanting to change

the subject to anything other than her thoughts, the
Jogger initiated a conversation about something she
hoped was a safe topic: the children.

THE JOGGER: How old are your kids?
THE MOTHER: My daughters are thirteen and
    eight, and my son is eleven. Our eldest is
    eighteen, but he's at home doing his own
    thing. Do you have children?
THE JOGGER: Yes, I have three. My daughter
    is five and my sons are seven and two. How
    do you do it with four? We're finding it tough
    with our three at the moment. I can't imagine
    having to cope with more than that!

The Jogger flinched as a Frisbee came whooshing
past at close proximity.

THE MOTHER: Oh, it's certainly not easy. There
    have been plenty of ups and downs over the
    years, especially early on. My other half and
    I weren't really sure what we were doing at
    first.
THE JOGGER: Us too. It's like you come home
    from the hospital with them, and then all of
    a sudden you think to yourself, 'What am I
    supposed to do with them now?'
THE MOTHER: [laughing] Yeah, they definitely
    didn't come with a manual.
THE JOGGER: No. No, they didn't. And I don't
    know about you, but on top of that we had

so much conflicting advice from friends, family and health professionals about what we 'should' be doing. I know they were all trying to be helpful, it's just that in the end it was more confusing than anything else.

The Jogger's shoulders slumped as she stared up at the clouds for a moment. Parenting could often be completely overwhelming, let alone during a pandemic. She recalled the morning and her inglorious storming into the front room.

THE MOTHER: Yes, we definitely had a similar experience, and still do really. Everybody has an opinion, but it's just something we've learned to deal with over the years. What about you guys? How did you do it? How did you make sense of it all so that you could raise your kids as best you could?

The mother had given up offering the Jogger fruit by this point and was instead applying hand sanitiser, preparing to tuck into a banana.

THE JOGGER: I guess we just treated everything as suggestions or possible options, but not definite truths. Then we tried things out until we found what worked for us as a family.
THE MOTHER: That makes sense. I don't think we really noticed it at first, that we were actually making our way through it. It just sort

of hit us one day. What was it for you? How did you know when you'd 'got it' and that things were working for you?

THE JOGGER: Usually we knew something was helpful because my partner and I would start to communicate better. We talked more. Well, I say that – we used our phones a lot more, actually.

The Jogger laughed to herself; this was bringing back fond memories. She started to recall some of the photos they'd exchanged, such as when the children fell asleep in ridiculous places, and, of course, those precious videos when the kids would say or do something new.

THE JOGGER: We ended up sending each other messages on our phones so that we knew when they'd had their last feed or nappy change or nap. That way we knew what was happening, and we didn't have to worry about remembering it all – especially when we weren't sleeping very much.

THE MOTHER: That's brilliant! I wish we'd done that. We tried to write everything down in a notebook. As you can imagine, that didn't always work at two in the morning when you're holding a crying baby. I'll bet that made a huge difference for you both.

The mother took a bite of her banana as roars of

laughter erupted from her children playing nearby.

THE JOGGER: For me and my partner it meant
   that we didn't have to think so much about
   everything because we had it written down in
   our phones.
THE MOTHER: What did you do then, when
   you didn't have to think so much?
THE JOGGER: I think we were able to just
   relax more and then take things as they came
   without worrying so much.
THE MOTHER: I'll bet! It's such a huge thing,
   isn't it, just being able to relax. What do you
   think your eldest would have noticed about
   you and your partner when you were both
   relaxed and taking things as they came?

The mother shifted a bit closer to the Jogger and
leaned forward so she wouldn't miss a word.

THE JOGGER: You're really testing my memory
   now! I guess he would have noticed that we
   were smiling more, interacting with him
   more, laughing and playing with him and the
   toys he loved so much.
THE MOTHER: What sort of toys were his
   favourite?
THE JOGGER: He had one of those colourful
   fabric books. Each page would make that
   scrunching, rustling sound when you
   squeezed it or moved it – just hearing it meant

that I could stop for a minute, as I knew he'd
be happy playing with it for a while. He loved
that thing. He always had it with him, mostly
in his mouth, and we always tried to read it to
him and look at what was on the pages.

THE MOTHER: [laughing] Yeah, ours chewed
on anything they could get their hands on!
What was your son like when you were
reading him that book?

THE JOGGER: He would do that thing where he
looked at the book like he was seeing it for the
first time, and then he'd laugh as he went to
chew it again.

The mother clapped her hands with amusement, her
smile widening as she nodded knowingly.

THE MOTHER: What did you do when he did
that?

THE JOGGER: We just laughed with him and
kept playing.

THE MOTHER: Sounds like it was a lovely time.

THE JOGGER: Yes, it really was.

THE MOTHER: And being able to figure things
out and have lovely times like those, how did
that influence the two of you as you carried
on working through the ups and downs of
parenting?

Just then a plodding but determined runner trundled
past the benches, red-faced and breathing heavily.

Both the mother and the Jogger turned away
momentarily, careful to avoid the man's coughs and
splutters.

THE JOGGER: Figuring things out was great.
It made us feel like we could do it *and* enjoy
doing it, rather than just thinking of it as a
chore or a task. That we could enjoy life at the
same time. Thinking about it, we always have
times like that, but then something happens
and you have to figure it out all over again.
THE MOTHER: Yes, it's definitely a rollercoaster.
I know for us as soon as we thought we had it
all figured out things changed again. How old
did you say your eldest is now? Six? Seven?
THE JOGGER: Seven.
THE MOTHER: And you have two younger
ones?
THE JOGGER: Yes, they're five and two.

The mother shuffled to face the Jogger, tilting her
head in thought, the half-eaten banana on the bench
now entirely forgotten.

THE MOTHER: So you've been doing this for
seven years, and with another two children
along the way. How did you keep going until
you found the things that worked for you all?
THE JOGGER: That's a tough one. I have no
idea.

She stared into the distance for a moment. Waiting patiently, the mother sat perfectly still as she gave the Jogger space to contemplate her answer.

THE JOGGER: I suppose we just keep going. We work through the tough times knowing that we're doing our best, and if things don't go particularly well, then we can talk about it and try again the next time. Neither of us is perfect, and we seem to have grown to appreciate that in our family.

THE MOTHER: What helps you to keep going through the tough times?

THE JOGGER: We have those moments when you see things working. It sounds silly, but I'll often be stressing out over the way I said something or thinking about what I could have done differently in a particular situation. And then it's like the kids have totally moved on from it, because they're asking me to play again or running over and giving me a cuddle. You know?

THE MOTHER: Absolutely.

The sounds of the children playing echoed as the clouds shifted and sunlight burst down on the park.

THE JOGGER: How did we get to talking about all this?

THE MOTHER: [laughing] I'm not sure. I suppose it's like life in general, especially during this pandemic.

THE JOGGER: What do you mean?

THE MOTHER: Well, I don't know about you, but I've really struggled with this whole COVID situation, especially the pressures of being a parent.

THE JOGGER: You're definitely not alone there.

THE MOTHER: Trying to plan anything has been a nightmare, and I know I was at a point where I was so busy and worried about what's next or what's going wrong that I often forgot about the things I was already doing that are good for me and my family. Things that are working for us. And I know when I've looked at what's working, it's helped me to keep going and feel like I can face whatever comes next.

THE JOGGER: You're right. I'm going to write that down. Thank you!

The Jogger started to type into her phone.

we're already doing things that are working for us

THE MOTHER: You're welcome. Right, I need to get the kids home now. My husband and I have this online quiz tonight, and I have a thousand things to do before then. It's been nice talking with you.

THE JOGGER: And you. Thank you for those

questions. They really got me thinking about things in a new way.

The mother left, collecting her half-eaten banana and bottle of hand sanitiser while calling her children to follow her. The Jogger returned to her phone. Still no reply from her partner, but the message had been read. Energised by the memories she had just discussed, she sent another message.

> Do you remember how we used to work together when the kids were little? Everything was absolutely crazy, but we made it through. I want to get back to that. I mean, some of that. We can leave the sleepless nights in the past!

As she held her phone, the Jogger paused, taking in her surroundings and savouring the moment. Various birds were sitting in the trees, their chirping lingering on the breeze. As she turned to see where the nearest sound was coming from, her attention was drawn to a tree where a starling sat on a branch, singing to itself.

The grey clouds continued to move across the sky, parting sporadically to reveal a blue canvas and shimmering yellow sun.

Collecting her thoughts, the Jogger took several steady deep breaths. These moments of appreciating her surroundings brought her back to that drawing Aiden had given her and the conversation with the dog walker. This is exactly what they'd talked about doing.

It's just like the mother said – I'm doing things already. There are signs of my hopes and of the future I would like to see happening all around me.

The cheerful sound of a bicycle bell interrupted her thoughts. She slid her feet out of the way just in time as a smiling family of four rode past. Seeing the upbeat cyclists, the Jogger recalled more of the conversation with the mother. It focused on what they were doing well as parents, what was working and remembering a time when this had happened. Even though the Jogger was aware that she hadn't made it very far in her run, she couldn't help but think, 'What else am I doing already?'

Lightly drumming her fingers on the arm of the park bench, she thought back to her conversation with Bill. What are my hopes? To relax and move forward with my life. Then, keeping this in mind, she revisited the questions the mother had asked.

What else am I doing to move forward with my life?

I suppose I made it out for a run this morning. And yesterday I did manage to do some schoolwork with my kids.

She recalled how she'd sat down with her children and played shopkeeper with the two older ones to help with maths. Her daughter was the shopkeeper with items for sale, which were toys and bits and pieces from the cupboards in the kitchen. The Jogger wrote out little Post-it Notes with prices for each item and gave the children some real money from the pot of coins in the front room.

But how did I do it?
I guess it was something more fun and interactive, instead of sitting down and having to write or watching something educational, which didn't work for us before.

What was I doing when this was happening?
I was able to have fun with the children, ask questions and just relax. I didn't have to worry about everything else, I could just be there with them.

What were they doing?
They were laughing and having fun. They seemed calmer and happier as they worked together to figure out how much money was needed, what the value of the coins were and how much change to give.

What did I do after that?

*I was able to have more fun. What did I do?
Ha, that's right. I brought my youngest into it and
said to them, 'Don't forget about your brother. He
needs to buy something too.' So they carried on
playing and 'shopping' for him as well.*

What impact did that have on all of us?

*It meant that we all had fun playing together,
while also learning about money and doing some
maths. And it really made me feel like I was doing
a good job as a parent.*

At this point, the Jogger realised that it was
completely true – she was already doing things that
were helping her to move forward with her life.

Feeling lighter and more optimistic, she stood
with her head held higher and her shoulders back.
She set off again – this time with swift, purposeful
strides.

Activity/Exercise:

Thinking about your own life, consider the following
questions, just as the Jogger did.

What's already working?
(Feel free to make a list.)

How have you made these things work?

What are you able to do when things are working?

Who notices these things about you? What do they do in response to you?

How do you then respond to them?

What difference does it make to you and to them?

What efforts have you made that help to keep these things going?

FIVE

USE WHAT YOU HAVE

'We already have everything we
need.'

Pema Chödrön

The purposeful strides that the Jogger had set off
with were starting to fade a little, her legs beginning
to feel weary once more. As she slowed down, she
noticed a clearing with an inviting trail winding
through it, leading to what looked like ancient
woodland. Despite living in the area for a number
of years, the Jogger had never really noticed this
particular trail before, nor the wood it led to. She
seemed to have noticed more places like this since
the first lockdown, and this one definitely looked like
a hidden gem worth exploring. Starting to become
aware of how far she was from home, she decided to
make her way through the wood anyway – for hidden
gems are not to be dismissed just because you feel a
bit tired.

Accepting the trail's invitation, the Jogger
breathed in the fresh air and ran her hands over the
rough bark of a tree. Wildflowers filled every crevice
between larger plants, illuminating the scene with
colour. Even this curious detour was not immune
to the Jogger's beeping watch as it flashed the time,

alerting her to how she had lost track of where she was.

She came to a sudden stop and leaned against a fallen oak tree, clearly magnificent in its prime but now nothing more than a carcass – and the perfect seat for a tired runner. She lowered herself onto the trunk and tried to ignore her aching body. Mud was splattered on her shoes and legs, and the muscles in her calves throbbed. She definitely needed a break – and probably a nap. After taking several deep breaths, she surveyed the route ahead.

Beyond the fallen oak lay a crossroads: one path widened and appeared to be popular with joggers, judging by the well-worn track; the other was signposted as a public footpath. It looked untamed, with overgrown foliage on either side making the trail fit for only the thinnest of ramblers. Grass peeked through the dirt where boots had trampled. The Jogger supposed this must be part of a longer hiking route – a route she would usually stay far away from. It wasn't that she was against the idea of a full day's hike, only that she was struggling to run even 5K.

She settled more comfortably on the oak and started to catch her breath. Pulling out her phone, she saw there was still no reply to her messages. Then all of a sudden three little dots appeared. Her partner was obviously typing something. As quickly as they appeared, the dots were gone. The Jogger waited. Nothing. 'Oh, come on,' she thought, before remembering that he was at home with the kids, so it shouldn't be surprising that there hadn't been a response.

Other members of the public began to pass by. Some had fancy tracking equipment and running gear, others did not, but all of them seemed to be in better shape than the Jogger. Before she could feel too envious and sorry for herself, she noticed movement on the narrow trail. A hiker emerged from the dense foliage.

He wore sturdy leather boots and a tiny backpack slung over one shoulder. With a cautious look he asked for permission to sit on the tree trunk. The Jogger was happy to make an inviting gesture, as there was more than enough space for two, even considering social distancing. The hiker responded with a grateful nod as he sat down.

As with many conversations between strangers, this one started with talking about the weather.

THE JOGGER: It's a really nice day today, isn't it?
THE HIKER: Definitely. It was pretty cool and
    cloudy this morning but it's warming up a
    little now.

THE JOGGER: How far have you been walking?
THE HIKER: I think I'm about eight miles on
from when I last checked my phone.

The Jogger let out an audible gasp; the hiker seemed
far too laid-back and upbeat for someone who had
already walked at least eight miles.

THE JOGGER: Wow! What are you doing
hiking eight miles? Keeping yourself in shape,
or … ?
THE HIKER: I'm planning a long-distance
charity walk. And if you think eight miles
is long, it's going to be just over fifteen in
the end. I've been staying active during the
pandemic by getting into charity walks. It's a
great way to support people and stay healthy.
THE JOGGER: That sounds like a great idea.
Which charity is this walk for?
THE HIKER: It's an organisation in my area that
I've been so touched and inspired by. They're
fundraising for young refugees who have been
through some of the toughest situations you
could imagine. It's simply amazing how these
youngsters work through such challenging
circumstances and still make the most of every
opportunity. I wanted to find a way to support
them and the charity, so organising this walk
seemed like the least I could do.

A crack and a snap indicated that part of the decaying

oak was giving way, and the Jogger moved to a safer position.

THE JOGGER: I think I've seen this initiative on
 social media. I was so moved by the stories
 of those young refugees, but I didn't know
 if there was a way of supporting the charity
 other than by donating money, which I'm
 rather short of at the moment. I'll definitely
 look into your sponsored walk and will try to
 sign up once it's all set up. I'm not sure if I can
 do fifteen miles though!
THE HIKER: Yeah, it is a bit of a distance, but
 that's why I'm hoping to organise it to include
 places just like this, where people can rest
 for as long as they need to. I wouldn't expect
 anyone to walk the whole distance in one go,
 but many will sign up with the intention of
 finishing and supporting the charity, even if
 they rest at every opportunity. And it's the
 intention that counts, right?

The Jogger nodded in agreement, and noticed herself silently adding: 'Yes, and also the hope.'

The hiker opened his backpack and pulled out a bottle of water, a map, a notebook with the name 'Kamal' written on the front, and what the Jogger would describe as a small picnic: a sandwich wrapped in foil, a container filled with a mix of nuts and seeds, a flapjack, a chocolate bar, a banana and a couple of oranges. She wondered what else he could possibly have in his tiny backpack.

The hiker opened a side pouch to reveal a small bottle of hand sanitiser, a mask, a mini first-aid kit and, finally, a pen. Since it seemed he'd produced all these things out of nowhere, it made the Jogger think of Hermione's bag in the Harry Potter books, which somehow held far more than you would think possible and always produced whatever was needed.

THE JOGGER: You seem to be extremely well prepared, given how tiny your backpack is. I can't believe how much you can fit in there.

THE HIKER: I know what you mean. It gives the impression of being so small, doesn't it? It took me a while to learn how and what to put in it so it has everything I need without being too heavy, especially over long distances. You wouldn't want to drag stuff around with you that you don't need, would you?

THE JOGGER: I think I'd struggle to keep it to a minimum. Whenever I go on a trip I pack way too much, for those 'just in case' moments. How do you do it?

THE HIKER: Well, everybody brings what they feel they need when they set out on a journey. For some people that's a lot, and for others not as much – it's different for everyone. As for me, I realised I don't need as much because I already have other skills and abilities that I can use to get through most situations. As well as our physical backpacks, we're all

carrying an invisible backpack full of our own
personal resources.

The Jogger felt a shiver when she heard the hiker
say, 'I already have other skills and abilities that I can
use to get through most situations.' She made a firm
mental note, which she would later add to her phone:
this was a pearl of wisdom she didn't want to forget.
Something was shifting. Somehow the hiker's words
complemented what the mother in the park had
said about discovering that much of what you were
hoping for was already happening.

THE HIKER: Mind you, I see you're not carrying
that much with you. A lot of joggers bring all
sorts of things with them, but you don't seem
to have nearly as much.
THE JOGGER: I didn't think I'd run this far. I
just sort of got carried away, and now I wish
I'd brought a few things with me, like a bottle
of water. I'm not even completely sure where I
am right now.
THE HIKER: Well, you must have packed some
sort of backpack that has got you here, even if
it's not a physical one.

The hiker closed his eyes and breathed deeply,
as though he'd just caught the fragrance of the
wildflowers.

THE JOGGER: What do you mean?

A puzzled expression had crossed her face.

THE HIKER: Maybe you're already carrying
everything you need – it just isn't in the form
of a physical backpack.

The Jogger dug into her pockets. It didn't seem there
was any wisdom or conscious planning behind what
she found.

THE JOGGER: I don't have much, only my house
keys and my phone. I'm not really sure where
you're going with this.

THE HIKER: OK, think back to what I told
you about the refugees supported by the
charity. They've been through really difficult
circumstances, and ultimately their situation
doesn't always get better. These youngsters
somehow just make a choice to call on the
resources they do have – like their strength,
determination and sense of humour.

THE JOGGER: And their courage too.

THE HIKER: Exactly. They didn't get through
the tough challenges because of the tangible
possessions or supplies they had. It's because
of their backpack full of intangible skills – the
abilities and resources that they developed
over time, or had to develop because of the
terrible situations they found themselves
in. And while physical resources can often
be helpful, we also have valuable skills and

abilities in our own inner backpacks.

THE JOGGER: OK, I think I'm starting to follow you now, Kamal.

The hiker looked startled.

THE HIKER: How did you know my name?
THE JOGGER: I saw it written on your notebook.
THE HIKER: [laughing] Well, you definitely have the skill of observation!

He took a swig of water before returning to his previous point.

THE HIKER: I'm learning to trust my inner backpack more and more, and it's been especially useful during these uncertain times. So how about you? What have you brought with you today in your invisible backpack that you didn't even know you'd packed?

The Jogger's brow furrowed as the hiker took a big bite of his sandwich. His gaze held steady as he watched her carefully.

THE JOGGER: Ummmm…

The hiker paused to swallow.

THE HIKER: I know. We usually think about

what we've left behind and what we haven't
packed – like you said, you wished you'd
brought a bottle of water – and we forget
what we've already got. So, come on, have a
go. What do you think you packed today that
other people can't easily see?

THE JOGGER: I have no idea. Sorry.

THE HIKER: That's all right, it's tough to
think about these things. Maybe if I ask you
something different instead. What do you
already know about yourself that tells you
you're going to make it home, even though
you haven't got that bottle of water and aren't
sure where you are?

THE JOGGER: I just know that I will. No
problem.

THE HIKER: That's interesting. It could be a
problem to some, I imagine, but it's not a
problem for you. What does that 'knowing
that you will' tell you about yourself?

THE JOGGER: I guess I'm good at working
through uncertainty. Is that a skill?

The Jogger smiled to herself; she had dealt with a fair
amount of uncertainty on this run already, what with
all the unusual interactions along the way. But the
hiker was persistent and wouldn't leave it at that.

THE HIKER: OK. And how did you become
good at working through uncertainty so that
it's not a problem?

THE JOGGER: I guess it's a choice, isn't it?
And I was able to make that choice because I
trust myself enough. I trust in my skills and
abilities, so I can be somewhat OK with being
uncertain.

THE HIKER: That sounds really cool. Out of
curiosity, and forgive me if I'm being too
nosy, but which skills and abilities do you
think have been most useful in being OK with
uncertainty? That could be something I could
use too!

The Jogger chuckled at the hiker's persistence.
Noticing a shoelace had come undone, she reached
down to retie it, buying some time to formulate her
answer.

THE JOGGER: Glad to be of help if I can, but
just give me a second … I think it's my ability
to influence certain aspects of a situation –
not necessarily changing the situation itself,
but adapting how I think about it. I know
that I can change my mood when I notice I'm
beginning to overthink. Not that I use this
ability as often as I'd like.

THE HIKER: So you've cultivated the skills of
influencing and changing your thinking and
mood if you choose to?

THE JOGGER: I'd like to think so.

Another runner tore past and down the open path,

dressed in colour-coordinated sports gear and equipped with multiple gadgets, including expensive-looking headphones. Distracted for only the briefest moment, the hiker returned to the conversation.

THE HIKER: That's great. I think I might want to learn some of that too. If you don't mind sharing, what differences have those skills and abilities made when you chose to use them?

THE JOGGER: A massive difference. I was able to move from where I didn't want to be to a place that felt better. Like for instance, the other week when my partner had a really bad day at work and started to vent about it. I recognised that his frustrations weren't because of me, so I didn't take it personally. I responded calmly and listened to what happened until he calmed down.

THE HIKER: I see. And what impact did that have on you afterwards?

THE JOGGER: He thanked me for it later on, and said how helpful it had been for him. We were then able to have a good evening and enjoy each other's company. I felt lighter, able to trust myself and more hopeful. I was so pleased that I didn't let his mood get to me when it easily could have.

THE HIKER: And, if you don't mind me asking just one more question, when you feel lighter, able to trust yourself and more hopeful, what difference does that make?

The Jogger thought hard. There was that 'difference' question again. She'd heard it several times today, but, interestingly, it always produced a different answer.

> THE JOGGER: It's a huge relief to know that I don't need to do more than I already am. That I am enough. I can just carry on doing things rather than overthinking them.
>
> This sense of lightness and trust in myself tells me that I already have the right skills and abilities to help shift my mood. I've used them before, so why not use them again? They're in my backpack, as you say. I wish I could remind myself of that more often.

The hiker stood up to leave and began to pack his things away. The Jogger noticed a map of the local area and asked to take a look. A good decision, as the map revealed she was not far from a street she recognised. Leaving the fallen oak tree behind, the Jogger and the hiker warmly exchanged goodbyes, like only strangers with friend potential can, and went their separate ways.

The Jogger thought of her backpack filled with her particular skills, abilities and resources and wondered what size this backpack would be. Her thoughts returned to earlier in the day when she was first leaving home. Standing at her front door, she would never have believed she had an inner backpack.

At that point, all she could think about was what was going wrong and what she wasn't able to do. She would have thought it was more important to improve where she wasn't succeeding. Now she was less sure about this. What good did it do to focus on the skills she didn't yet have? Right now, it certainly felt better to remember: 'I already have other skills and abilities that I can use to get through most situations.' Her backpack undoubtedly existed – and it had the potential to expand.

Opening her phone again, the Jogger wanted to share this feeling with her partner. Looking at her existing resources was refreshing, empowering and, surprisingly, gave her confidence that progress was possible.

> Random, but how on earth have we made it this far through all this covid business? It's been months and months, and we're still here. How have we done it?

She noticed a renewed spring in her step as she headed towards the edge of the wood; speaking to the hiker had been hugely encouraging. Updating the notes on her phone, the Jogger really wanted to test this idea of focusing on resources by asking someone else these questions. She felt a sudden urge to see if it could make a difference to other people in the same way it had to her.

As the Jogger made her way towards the street she'd identified on the hiker's map, she caught the aroma of freshly ground coffee. She followed its call. As the smell became stronger, the outskirts of the wood revealed a small café. She was pleasantly surprised to see that this local business was still up and running despite the continual changes and economic uncertainty.

She approached the café, which was offering hot and cold drinks and home-made cakes via an improvised window – takeaways only. She was relieved to see that not only could she pay with her phone, but the whole place was set up to be as safe as possible. The serving window had a Plexiglas covering, and there was hand sanitiser next to the napkins on the little counter. Temporary markers on the ground indicated where customers should queue to stay a safe distance apart. After some hesitation, the Jogger decided to treat herself to a piece of cake, and perhaps see if she could practise asking the hiker's questions to the person operating the till.

There was no one in the queue as she approached the window. Behind the Plexiglas was a barista absorbed in a Sudoku puzzle. It was difficult to make out how old she was; perhaps the same age as the Jogger or maybe a little older. As she thought about ordering a bottle of water, she surveyed the list of cakes written in chalk on the blackboard. When the barista looked up from her puzzle, the Jogger had the strange feeling that she knew her, but it took a moment to figure out where from.

It turned out they had met before, not often enough to become friends, but always in the same place and usually on the same day. The woman, whose name was Suzi, used to go to the same nail salon as the Jogger, which was why she didn't instantly recognise her as a barista.

SUZI: Hey, how are you doing? It's been ages since I've seen you.

THE JOGGER: Hi, I didn't expect to see you here. I'm good. How have you been?

SUZI: I've been OK, thanks. See anything you like on the blackboard? I've got everything except the Strawberry Dream. All the cakes are home-made, I know the baker personally and can highly recommend him.

THE JOGGER: Hmm, I'm supposed to be on a run, but I guess I can have a small piece of that chocolate cake.

SUZI: Good choice. That's usually what I go for.

Drink?

THE JOGGER: Just a bottle of water, please. So how long have you been working here?

SUZI: Not that long. It was usually my husband who'd be rattling around this place, but he's … no longer here.

THE JOGGER: Oh, I see, what's he doing now?

Suzi went quiet as she turned to get the cake and water.

SUZI: Well … he caught the virus, and … I lost him during the first wave. We didn't even manage to have a proper funeral for him because of the restrictions, and now all I've got left is this café…

THE JOGGER: Oh my goodness. I'm so very sorry to hear that, Suzi. I can't imagine how you must feel or what you've been through.

Suzi's eyes welled up with tears. The Jogger felt helpless to comfort her from the other side of the Plexiglas barrier. Wiping the tears away and brushing herself down, Suzi pulled herself together and cleared her throat.

SUZI : It's OK, I'm getting used to it.

She placed the cake and water on the counter.

SUZI: Here you go. I hope you enjoy it. And

please don't worry, I'm slowly finding a way to
carry on.

The Jogger fumbled for a napkin as she searched for
something appropriate to say.

THE JOGGER: Thank you, how much do I owe
you?
SUZI: That'll be £4.50, sorry that the prices are
so high. I've done the maths over and over,
and with the reduced income and all the extra
expenses, these are the prices I have to charge.
THE JOGGER: Don't worry, I completely
understand. And I hope this is OK, but would
you mind if I asked you a few questions that
might be of some help? I'd normally give you
a big hug, but since we can't do that, this is the
next best thing I can think of.
SUZI: Sure. That'd be nice.

The Jogger glanced down at the notes on her phone
as Suzi took a moment to pour herself a coffee.

THE JOGGER: OK, forgive me if this sounds
a bit strange, but given everything that's
happened, how have you kept going?
SUZI: Well, it's my choice to be here. I know
that my husband loved this business and I'm
determined to keep it afloat, even though
lots of other places are having to close. It's
been so tough, and I haven't had much help

because the finances won't allow me to hire anyone else full-time. I just try to focus on the parts of the work I enjoy, such as interacting with customers and organising everything in minute detail. Being here keeps me busy, helps me enjoy life a little bit more.

Suzi swept up some crumbs from her work surface, a content smile on her face.

THE JOGGER: Gosh, I wish I had even an ounce of your resilience and determination. Do you mind me asking where you learned to be like that ?

SUZI: To be honest, I'm surprised too! I never thought of myself as being resilient or determined. Thinking about it now, I suppose I've always had a stubborn streak when it comes to the really important things. If the café does close, it certainly won't be because I haven't tried everything I can to stop that from happening. I want to carry on the work that my husband invested so much time and effort in.

The Jogger looked up from her chocolate cake, licking icing from her fingers.

THE JOGGER: Well, I'm certainly glad that you're here, this cake is just what I needed. And I'm sure your husband would be proud to see the café still going.

SUZI: Thank you, that means a lot.

THE JOGGER: Is it OK if I ask a couple more questions?

SUZI: Of course.

THE JOGGER: What difference do your organisational skills, resilience and determination make to you?

SUZI: I suppose they help me to stay calmer, despite what's going on around me. They help me to believe that I will get through this, one way or another.

For a moment, Suzi looked like she had just spotted something rather wonderful, as if she was surprised and reassured to hear herself saying these things. She stood a little bit taller and her smile grew a little wider. Just then, the Jogger noticed a family walking towards the café, so she decided to say goodbye and leave Suzi to her thoughts.

THE JOGGER: It looks like you have some more customers on the way. I think I should be heading off now.

SUZI: They're not stopping just yet, I can tell. They'll take their time to decide whether to come closer or not. If you could give me a sec, I have an idea. There was a time, long ago, when I used to bake cakes myself. I was able to produce more than ten different variations of the chocolate cake you seem to have quite enjoyed. I would measure all the ingredients to the exact milligram and blend them to perfection. I wish I'd written down the recipes at the time.

She reached for a nearby notepad and pen.

SUZI: I love working with numbers and figures. Would you mind if I scribble down some of the questions from our conversation, but in a way that makes sense to me? It will only take a couple of minutes. Can I offer you some coffee, and would you like to try another cake in the meantime? On the house. Maybe that'll encourage the family over there to come and get some too.

THE JOGGER: OK then, thanks. Happy to be of help if it'll get you more customers. I'll go with your recommendation on the cake this time.

As Suzi handed over a generous slice of New York cheesecake, the Jogger looked more closely at her. It was strange. When the woman was talking about her various resources, such as her resilience and determination, she seemed to visibly change. With so much going on in her life, it was almost as if she'd forgotten about the skills she'd utilised on a daily basis. Being reminded of those skills had revealed a different version of Suzi. Her eyes shone as she busily scribbled, and there was a passion in the way she was swirling the pen across the page. A passion she had obviously experienced at other times in her life. The layer of dust that had been covering that passion vanished as she finished the final line with a flourish.

SUZI: Here we are, what do you think?

She showed her a drawing of a 1 to 10 scale with a list of questions following it. The Jogger read the questions, and the ideas were indeed interesting.

THE JOGGER: Would you mind if I took a snapshot of this?
SUZI: By all means, go ahead. I would have given it to you, but it's something I'd like to hang onto.

The Jogger took a snapshot, and just as she was about to say something more, the family that had been hovering nearby decided to approach. It was time to go.

THE JOGGER: Thanks again for the cake. All the best to you and your family. I'll be thinking of you, and hopefully see you again soon. Maybe when the nail salon reopens?
SUZI: Thanks, yes, I'm looking forward to it! Stay safe.

Walking from the café, the Jogger opened her phone to save the photo of Suzi's scale alongside her notes about inner backpacks from the conversation with the hiker. When she finished, she found herself contemplating one line in particular: 'I already have other skills and abilities that I can use to get through most situations.' As she looked up from her phone, just before deciding which direction to take home, she recognised the truth in its words. Although often easily forgotten, the Jogger really did have the resources to overcome most situations. Her final thoughts, together with the notes made by Suzi, were as follows:

Activity/Exercise

The Hiker's backpack.

Think about your own backpack of resources, skills, abilities and qualities. What are they?

> How have you learned these skills?
>
> Where have these qualities come from?
>
> Which of them do you think will be most useful in your current challenges?
>
> In what ways are they going to be useful?

Suzi's scaling questions:

> On a scale from 1 to 10, where 10 is your absolute confidence that you can overcome your current challenge and 0 is the opposite, where are you now?
>
> What are ten things already happening that make your score as high as it is and not lower?

Which skills and abilities have been helpful in getting all the way up to that score? How have those skills and abilities been helpful?

When you have thoroughly explored your existing resources, look for signs of progress:

If you moved up your scale by one point, what would that look like?

What else would be happening at one point up on the scale?

What would you notice about yourself once you've moved up one point on the scale?

Who else would notice that you were one point higher?

And what would they notice about you?

What else would they notice about you?

How would you know that they have noticed you being one point higher?

And what difference would it make to you that they have noticed?

If you feel you are finding these questions challenging, don't worry – they are unusual and take practice. Keep repeating the process of asking yourself all these questions and you will soon master them.

SIX

FROM COPING TO CREATING

'May your choices reflect your
hopes, not your fears.'
Nelson Mandela

With various thoughts whirling around in her head, the Jogger sped up a little, determined to finish her run. Despite the uneven pavement of a residential road not far from home, she was just getting into her stride when she heard her phone ping. A message had come through. Hoping it might be from her partner, she stopped to check it.

It wasn't her partner. It was her friend Jacob. She and Jacob had been friends since their schooldays. Jacob had been struggling lately. Lockdowns, restrictions on socialising and having to go through a recent period of self-isolation due to possibly having COVID-19 had really taken their toll on him, especially since he lived on his own. Despite everything she had on her plate, the Jogger tried to stay in touch with him to offer moral support.

JACOB: [text] You are not going to believe this. It's been two weeks since I finished self-isolating.

I'm finally able to get back out into the world,
and now I have to self-isolate for another two
weeks! I don't know if I can do this again. You
free to talk?

THE JOGGER: [text] Oh no! That's terrible. I'm
just out for a run at the moment. Can I call you
later?

JACOB: Sorry to bug you while you're running.
Message me when you're free.

She felt bad about not speaking to him now, given
how difficult things have been for him lately, but she
also needed to make her way home. Then she had a
sudden thought.

THE JOGGER: Actually, let me send you
something. I just had a conversation with
someone and I found it really useful. It might be
of some help to you too.

She sent Jacob the photo of Suzi's 1 to 10 scaling
questions and the follow-up questions about skills
and resources.

JACOB: Thanks. I'll have a look at it.
THE JOGGER: No worries. Speak later.

Just as she put her phone away, she heard her friend,
the gardener, calling her name. The Jogger sighed
to herself, wondering if she would ever get home.
The gardener was one of her oldest friends in the

neighbourhood, so she couldn't pass by without stopping for a minute or two. She made her way over to him, stopping at a safe social distance.

The gardener was on his hands and knees tending his immaculate plot of land. It was only a narrow front garden, yet he had made the space his own. A trimmed hedge without so much as a leaf out of place surrounded the garden. There were two patches of soil: one along the right side of the path and the other perpendicular to it. The earth was dark and damp without a weed in sight and some of the plants and shrubs were in bloom.

The Jogger saw that the gardener was surrounded by books and tools, some of which she had never seen before. There was a hand tool that looked almost like a flower with a diamond-shaped tip; something that reminded her of the pop-up play tunnels that her kids had in the garden; and some sort of miniature chemistry set. The Jogger was curious.

THE JOGGER: What are all these things for?
THE GARDENER: The books are for researching different types of plants and...

He reached for a small leather notebook bursting at the seams. Its edges were worn and half-loose pages stuck out haphazardly.

THE GARDENER: ... this is where I keep my notes about the things I've learned from different jobs. That curved tool over there is my weeder and cultivator. It's fantastic for weeding as well as loosening up the soil before transplanting things from the greenhouse to the garden.
THE JOGGER: And what about the tunnel over there? Isn't that for kids?
THE GARDENER: No. That's called a row cover. It helps to protect the plants from too much sun when it's hot and from frost when it's cold.
THE JOGGER: What about those vials over there?
THE GARDENER: That kit is for testing the pH and chemical make-up of the soil.

The Jogger's brow furrowed.

THE JOGGER: I thought gardening was mostly
    putting stuff in the ground, watering it and
    pulling out weeds?
THE GARDENER: [laughing] Sure – sometimes
    it is.
THE JOGGER: I know I'm no professional, but
    that's all I ever do.

A knowing smile broadened across the gardener's
face. He had seen his friend's improvised garden
many times and the Jogger was right: she was
definitely not a professional horticulturist.

THE GARDENER: It all depends on what you
    want and how you want things to be.

That sentence really stood out for the Jogger. It
sounded so similar to what she'd heard from Bill and
the dog walker. Shaking her head, she looked down
at the pavement, thinking what an odd day this was
turning out to be. She lifted her head just in time to
reconnect with the gardener's gaze as he continued
his enlightening monologue.

THE GARDENER: There are a lot of things
    going on in a garden. The pH and chemical
    make-up of the soil will determine what will
    or won't grow there. Different plants need
    different amounts of water. And then there's
    companion planting. Have you heard of that?
THE JOGGER: I have no idea what that is.

THE GARDENER: It's all about planting certain things near each other that can help your plants or vegetables thrive. So, for instance, if you're trying to grow carrots, it's a good idea to grow spring onions nearby, because the smell of the spring onions helps to keep carrot flies away.

THE JOGGER: I had no idea there was so much to gardening.

The man was speaking with such fervent knowledge about his garden that the Jogger was completely absorbed. She had always known how seriously her friend took the maintenance of his precious land, but she had never thought about how much work went into keeping it perfectly in order. The gardener's enthusiasm was infectious, and the Jogger listened intently to his every word.

THE GARDENER: There is definitely a lot to it when you look into it closely. Gardening is not an exact science, since you never really know how things are going to turn out. That's why it takes constant effort and focus.

THE JOGGER: I understand the effort but I'm not sure about the focus.

THE GARDENER: I need to focus because so many different things are going on. I have to keep weeding, pruning, watering and so on, all the while looking for signs that everything is growing the way it should.

THE JOGGER: Let me see if I've got this
    right. So you use all these tools and all your
    knowledge to work out a plan to make things
    turn out just right?
THE GARDENER: Not quite. Even with
    everything I know, there are plenty of
    unpredictable problems – the weather, bugs,
    snails, foxes – that can totally ruin what I'm
    trying to grow. So I focus on doing everything
    I can along the way, and then watch for the
    signs I'm hoping to see, signs that tell me I'm
    on the right track.

The gardener stuck his trowel into the soil, then
gently inspected the vibrant petals of a nearby flower.

THE JOGGER: So you're looking for the signs
    that things are working and growing in a way
    you're hoping for?
THE GARDENER: Now you've got it. These
    are the things that keep me going. It's what
    tells me I'm doing something right and that
    everything is progressing. That's what I keep
    in that yellow and blue notebook over there –
    the signs of progress.

He pointed to his van, which was parked on the
driveway with the passenger door wide open; the
'signs of progress' notebook lay on a well-worn
leather seat, next to a box of disposable gloves.
    Stepping out of the way as a pedestrian walked

past, the Jogger once again shook her head in bemusement.

> THE JOGGER: Wouldn't you want to look out for what's going wrong so you can then fix things?
>
> THE GARDENER: I could. And, in fact, I did exactly that for a number of years. Guess what I learned as I was doing it that way?

Pushing himself up with a pitchfork and dusting soil from his shirt, the gardener glanced towards the sky. A few silvery clouds threatened to unleash rain.

> THE JOGGER: I have no idea. Perhaps you learned when you needed to do something in particular?
>
> THE GARDENER: Yes, it might have given me a bit of a warning about certain things, but I also spent a lot of time seeing my mistakes and my failures. Doing that taught me what not to do when gardening.
>
> THE JOGGER: You say that as if it's a bad thing.
>
> THE GARDENER: It turned out that it was, for me at least. I spent so much time focusing on the things I was getting wrong or the plants that weren't growing, that in the end I felt like I wasn't getting anything right. In fact, I almost thought about giving it all up. It was also taking up a lot of time, trying to figure out everything that wasn't working in order

not to miss something important. Then it struck me that I don't have the time to do all that, especially as there seemed to be no end to it.

This sounded crazy. The Jogger hadn't heard anything like this since someone told her that they actually worked faster by slowing down.

She'd always assumed that in order to figure things out and move forward, you first had to get to the bottom of what you were doing wrong.

THE JOGGER: So how did you turn it around?
THE GARDENER: I realised that mistakes were part of life, but ultimately it didn't help me figure out what I could be doing instead to actually help things grow. So I started paying more attention to and looking out for those little signs that told me what I was doing was encouraging everything to flourish. I just kept doing more of the things that showed signs of helping. And that's when it all clicked into place.
THE JOGGER: So rather than looking at what's not working, you started to look out for the possible signs that things *were* working – signs of progress rather than setbacks?
THE GARDENER: Exactly.

The Jogger's eyes shone with clarity.

THE JOGGER: Wow.

THE GARDENER: What is it?

THE JOGGER: It's just making me think about the other conversations I've had today. Lots of people have been saying similar things.

THE GARDENER: I'm not surprised. Looking at it this way has certainly changed things for me, and it works in so many situations. I mean, the other day I was talking with a friend who was feeling overwhelmed by everything, especially with all that's changed since this COVID business. He was trying to manage his mental health, find a job after being made redundant, and needing to pay the bills. So I asked what the smallest sign would be that he was moving forward with things.

THE JOGGER: And what did your friend say?

THE GARDENER: He said that he would be getting up earlier in the day.

THE JOGGER: But what does that have to do with anything?

THE GARDENER: I had no idea either at first. It's not like we were talking about getting somewhere on time. My friend then told me that if he woke up earlier, he would have more time in the day to finish all the jobs on his to-do list. And if he did that, he said it would make a massive difference, because at the moment he's sleeping in and losing half the day.

The Jogger squinted as a beam of sunlight bounced off the gardener's front window.

THE JOGGER: I guess that makes sense.
THE GARDENER: I know, right? I didn't get it after hearing his initial answer, but the more I think about it, the more I realise that it doesn't need to make sense to me. It's more important to make sense for him. It's put me off giving advice to people, because no matter how much experience I have, how am I to know what's going to be useful for them? So instead I stick to asking questions.

Seeing the potential value in this way of thinking, the Jogger pondered for a moment. The gardener softly hummed a tune as he started pruning a shrub.

THE GARDENER: So?
THE JOGGER: Huh?
THE GARDENER: So, if you've been talking with people about things like this already today, I'm guessing you're thinking about it right now? Come on, I know that look on your face!
THE JOGGER: Yeah, absolutely. I could tell you about all kinds of things that haven't been going well lately, and it's almost like I'm just waiting for the next thing to go wrong. So, of course, I'd rather look for something else to see what that could lead to.
THE GARDENER: And what might it be? We've

been friends long enough, so I know you're a good person and you're doing the best you can. So what would be the smallest sign that things were getting better for you?

Just then, the gardener's phone rang; it was a customer who had booked him for a job the following day.

THE GARDENER: I'm really sorry, I'm going to have to call them back in a minute. But before you go, let me give you something from my 'signs of progress' book.

He hurried to the yellow and blue notebook. Putting on a disposable glove, he tore out a page and handed it to the Jogger.

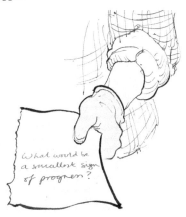

She gestured goodbye as the gardener put his phone to his ear. Glancing down at the torn page, the Jogger continued to think about his question. The smallest sign of progress? 'Well, maybe I'd spend more time with my partner in the evenings,' she thought, 'and maybe I'd ask if he wants to watch a film tonight.'

Just as she finished this thought, her phone vibrated. It was Jacob again.

JACOB: Hey, thanks for those questions. They've really got me thinking. Do you have any others?
THE JOGGER: Sure. What would be the smallest sign that things were getting better for you?

Expecting a reply from Jacob, she was happily surprised to finally get a message from her partner.

THE PARTNER: What kind of a run are you on? It's OK. We're all feeling it a bit right now. Talk more when you get home.
THE JOGGER: It's been a strange day. I'll definitely tell you all about it though!

As her smile spread wider than the Cheshire Cat's, the Jogger turned to make her way home.

Activity/Exercise:

Thinking about everything you have going on in your life, what would be the smallest sign that things were moving in the right direction for you and those around you?

SEVEN

WHAT HAS BEEN BETTER ALREADY?

'Be thankful for what you have;
you'll end up having more.'
Oprah Winfrey

The Jogger breathed in deeply through her nose
and stretched her arms wide, feeling light in spirit.
But her legs ached and spasmed with every step of
a journey that didn't seem to want to end. As the
day turned to a close, amber sunlight lingering, she
wished she didn't have to continue. Forget jogging –
even walking was a trial at this point.

Noticing that she now had better reception, the
Jogger stopped to check the map on her mobile and
searched for the quickest way home. In light of the
pandemic and ongoing restrictions, taking public
transport still felt risky; the thought of being trapped
in a small space, waiting for the sound of dreaded
coughing from the person sitting opposite was not
appealing. After some consideration, she wrestled
between calling an Uber and looking for another
solution – though none came to mind.

She found herself on a residential street with
well-kept semi-detached houses, their driveways

occupied by the types of car the Jogger would be proud to own: smart and sleek but not too flashy. It was the kind of street that would probably be considered rather lifeless during the day, but that certainly wasn't the case this evening. The sound of a loud and lively conversation between two residents calling to one another across the street rang through the air. Blushing and caught off guard for having come between them, the Jogger tried to make herself as invisible as possible, but it was too late. Crossing the road to join her friend, the female resident spotted the Jogger and waved.

THE RESIDENT: Hi! Are you all right?
THE JOGGER: Hi. I'm OK, thanks, just a bit
   tired from running … well, attempting to run
   anyway.

The woman laughed loudly.

THE RESIDENT: Eugh! I hate running! Rather
   you than me. My name's Jamie, by the way,
   and this is my friend Kwame.

Jamie pointed to a man in his forties sitting on a deckchair in his drive. Next to his feet was an open cooler box filled with ice and a six-pack of beer.

KWAME: Want one?

The Jogger hesitated, not only because it seemed counterintuitive to finish her run with an alcoholic beverage, but also because of COVID-19 precautions. Kwame acknowledged her caution.

KWAME: Don't worry, nobody's touched the bottles, only the cooler. Feel free to take one.

The Jogger gratefully took a bottle with ice-cold droplets running down its side.

JAMIE: I'm so sorry to hear about your job, Kwame. How are you doing?
KWAME: Thanks for asking. It's OK, I hated that job anyway.
JAMIE: What are you going to do next?
KWAME: I'll have to look into claiming benefits, I guess.

The Jogger picked at the label on the bottle, drifting in and out of the conversation and barely paying attention. Noticing her dreamlike state, the residents' interest turned to asking about the Jogger's day.

JAMIE: So, what about you? How was your run?

The genuine interest, coupled with the beer in her hand, was a warm reminder of how people had begun looking out for each other more since the pandemic started. Relaxing into the conversation, the Jogger embarked on the tale of her journey so far. The residents listened intently, and just as she was bringing her story to a close, Jamie raised her hand, prompting a rare pause in the conversation. Her smile was full of curiosity.

JAMIE: So, what's already been better?
THE JOGGER: How do you mean?
JAMIE: I mean, what's been better already today, since you've been learning all this stuff?

A puzzled expression overtook the Jogger's face as she tapped a finger against the beer bottle.

THE JOGGER: I have no idea ... I guess I was just taking it all in. It didn't occur to me to think about whether some things might *already* be better.

Kwame sipped his beer, evidently intrigued as he

watched Jamie persist with her question.

JAMIE: What do you think has changed so far?
Tell us about one or two things that have
already been better.

THE JOGGER: I've started to notice the things
around me more, and I've taken the time to
talk with people. I've been able to share some
useful questions, and I have a clearer idea
about some of the things I want in the future.

The signs were already clear without her trying to
make them happen. Two other interesting things
also occurred: her tiredness was fading and her legs
weren't aching anymore. The two residents were
completely engaged, their curiosity in the Jogger's
responses went beyond politeness – and rightly so:
her story, on the surface rather commonplace, was in
many ways fascinating. Obviously keen to know the
full extent of this story, they started to press for more
details.

JAMIE: What are some of the things you've
noticed around you?

THE JOGGER: The sounds of the birds in the
park, the wildflowers in the woodland and the
smell of freshly ground coffee from the café.

KWAME: And what about those questions you
said you'd been sharing? Where did they come
from?

THE JOGGER: From everyone I met today. I just

listened to the questions I found helpful and
shared them with other people.

KWAME: Like what?

THE JOGGER: Well, a minute ago, Jamie asked
me what's already been better. So, even
though it's a difficult situation for you, what's
already been better since you lost your job?

KWAME: OK, I see what you're doing here.

JAMIE: Go on, answer the question.

KWAME: It's been really stressful not knowing
where my next pay cheque is coming from,
but I also have a sense of freedom with it all.
It's like a blank canvas.

THE JOGGER: And what difference does that
make, having a sense of freedom and a blank
canvas?

KWAME: I suppose it's an opportunity. Maybe
now I can invest more time in myself and look
for a job that I'd feel passionate about.

He appeared pleasantly surprised with his answer.

KWAME: That was a good question.

THE JOGGER: Thanks, but it wasn't my
question, it was Jamie's.

JAMIE: Yeah, but you were the one who saw
the value in it and thought to repeat it to
Kwame.

The Jogger appreciated Jamie's compliment, and the
residents' overall interest in her story. They clearly

believed it was the Jogger herself who had made the
most of the day's conversations. It was the Jogger
who had done something about her situation. This
was a welcome and encouraging thought; if she'd
managed to make positive choices on a day like
today, maybe she could do it on other occasions too.
Could she do it whenever she chose to? She should
definitely add that to her notes later, she thought to
herself.

The Jogger finished her beer. She thanked the
residents for their curiosity and hospitality, and then
decided to walk home. Something was different,
something had changed, and the Jogger felt she
wasn't the same person who had started this journey
that morning. Yes, in some ways she was the same
old Jogger, with the same life struggles and worries,
but she had now discovered so many useful questions
along the way. She knew there was a version of
herself that she could draw from when she needed to.

Activity/Exercise:

Take a moment to reflect on your journey since you started reading this book.

What have you already learned?

What have you perhaps rediscovered?

And what has already been better since you started reading?

In thinking about it, allow yourself to think broadly:

What have you been noticing about yourself that is a sign you have learned something new? Or maybe rediscovered something you already knew?

· How have you learned that?

· What difference has this made?

· What new things have emerged for you?

· Who has noticed this?

· What have they been noticing?

· How do you know they have noticed?

What has been happening in your surroundings that has contributed to your learning and your new discoveries? How has this made a difference?

What else has enabled new things to emerge? And what has enabled your old wisdom to surface if you have rediscovered something you already knew?

If things continue in this direction as you carry on reading, what differences would you be hoping to notice?

Where would you notice them most?

EIGHT

A MIRACLE MINUTE

> 'All we have to decide is what to
> do with the time that is given
> us.'
> *Gandalf – The Lord of the Rings*

Her back ached and her feet were sore but the Jogger found herself smiling, physically exhausted yet somehow mentally refreshed. Finally, she had reached her home, after what had been a much longer and more eventful run than she had anticipated. Pausing at the brickwork path winding its way to the front door, she took out her keys and wondered what would be waiting for her inside. Perhaps before she went in it might help to check her notes quickly.

Taking out her phone, the Jogger reminded herself of everything she had learned, start to finish, from her encounters throughout the day:

1. Our hopes inspire our actions

· What are your best hopes from this situation?

· If those hopes were achieved, what difference would they make?

· What difference would those differences make?

·   If these hopes and differences were achieved, what
    might they lead to?

2. Think about what your life will be like once your
hopes are achieved, rather than how to achieve them

·   What will be the first sign that your hopes have
    come true?

·   What else will tell you that what you're hoping for
    has been achieved?

·   What will you notice about yourself that shows your
    hopes are present?

·   What will others notice?

·   How will they react?

·   How will you respond to their reaction?

·   What difference will that make?

·   Having achieved your hopes, what will please you
    most?

3. Find what's working already and do more of it

·   What's working?

·   How have you made it work?

- What are you able to do when things are working?

- What did others do in response to you?

- How did you then respond to them?

- What difference did it make?

- What efforts have you made that helped you to keep going?

4. I already have other skills and abilities that I can use to get through most situations

- On a scale from 1 to 10, where '10' is your absolute confidence that you can overcome your current challenge and '1' is the opposite, where are you now?

- What are ten things that make your score as high as that and not lower?

- Which skills and abilities have been helpful in getting all the way to that number on the scale? How did you utilise them?

5. Start to focus on possible signs that things are working

- Thinking about everything that you have going on in your life, what would be the smallest sign that things were moving in the right direction for you and those around you?

6. You can do it whenever you choose to

- What have you been doing yourself that fits with things being better already?

- How have you been doing that?

- What difference has this made?

- Who has noticed this?

- What have they been noticing?

- How do you know they have noticed?

- What have others been doing to make things better? What difference has this made to you?

- What has been happening in your surroundings that has contributed to things getting better?

- What else has enabled things to move towards being better?

- If things continued in this direction, what difference would you be hoping to notice?

Reaching the end of her notes, the Jogger paused, fumbling with the door keys. Taking a deep breath for courage, she decided to put her learning into practice. First up was Bill and his teaching on hopes. He had asked the Jogger what her best hopes were from her run.

She took a moment to ponder what her best hopes were for returning home.

> *To be happy and excited to be there. And what difference would being happy and excited to be there make? A more pleasant atmosphere.*

Exhaling slowly, the Jogger was already experiencing a renewed sense of optimism. She had a hope in mind now: a more pleasant atmosphere. Next, the dog walker and her future thinking. She would have asked: what will be the first sign that a more pleasant atmosphere is present?

> *The warmth of the welcome home.*

No doubt the dog walker wouldn't have stopped there, she would persist with further questions: what would the Jogger's family notice about her that showed her best hopes were present? How would the family react? And how will the Jogger respond to their reactions?

She relaxed her shoulders.

> *They'll notice how quick I am to apologise for my bad temper earlier. They'll be surprised! And grateful. How will I respond? With a heartfelt embrace.*

Smiling to herself, she recalled the difference question once more: what difference would a heartfelt embrace make?

We'll all feel closer again.

A half-laugh bubbled to the surface – she was actually looking forward to entering the house, something she hadn't felt so excited about in a long time. Scrolling through her notes, she looked for what the mother had told her: find what's already working and do more of it. The Jogger scuffed her shoe back and forth on the brick path as she searched for an answer.

The way that I make my partner laugh.

Her eyes shone with reminiscence. How had she made her partner laugh in the past? What difference did that make, and what efforts had she made to keep that going?

Putting on a funny voice and pulling a silly face always seems to work. It makes everyone laugh and things tend to calm down. It takes hard work to make others smile when I don't necessarily feel like smiling myself, but I've managed it before.

Twitching with anticipation, the Jogger was beginning to feel impatient. Whereas once the thought of returning home filled her with a mild anxiety, she was now feeling modestly confident

about it. She thought back to her encounter with
the hiker as she studied the next few points on her
phone: on a scale from 1 to 10, where '10' is absolute
confidence that you can overcome this current
challenge, and '1' is the opposite, where are you now?

Hmm ... a 5.

A car whizzed past with music blaring, but the Jogger
ignored it as she focused on the next question on the
list: what are the things that make your score as high
as this and not lower?

*Well ... I make my partner laugh, and I know
my two youngest kids will be delighted to see me,
no matter what happened earlier. I'm ready to
apologise and know what I want to say, and I'm
feeling better in myself already. And a big hug will
cheer up my eldest.*

She smiled to herself as she glanced down at the last
of her notes. These were the ones gleaned from her
good friend the gardener: what would be the smallest
sign that things were moving in the right direction?

*I'd knock on the door playfully rather than letting
myself in.*

Taking a step towards the door, the Jogger looked
at the typed notes one last time. What was it the
two residents had said? 'You can do it whenever you

choose to.' The Jogger couldn't agree more. Without looking at any further notes, she started living the moment.

Activity/Exercise:

Do you want to have a go at putting everything together for yourself? Try working through these questions and see how you get on.

1. What are your best hopes moving forward?

2. If those hopes were achieved, what difference would they make?

3. What will tell you within the first minute after finishing the book that your best hopes are somehow present?

4. What else will you notice about yourself that shows your best hopes are present?

5. Who will be the first person to notice that something is different?

6. What will they notice about you that shows your best hopes are present?

7. How will they react?

8. How will you respond to their reaction in a way that's in keeping with your best hopes?

9. What is something that's already working for you that shows this sort of future is possible?

10. In what ways have you contributed to making that something happen?

11. On a scale from 1 to 10, where '10' is absolute confidence you can achieve your best hopes, and '1' is the opposite, where would you place yourself?

12. What are five things already happening that allow you to score this high and not lower?

13. Which of your skills and abilities have been most helpful in attaining a score this high and not lower?

14. What would be the smallest sign that you were moving up one point on the scale?

15. If things continued in this direction, what difference would you be hoping to notice?

NINE

BEYOND COPING

'It is always hard to see
the purpose in wilderness
wanderings until after they are
over.'

John Bunyan

The Jogger and her family carried on with their lives,
not knowing how long the pandemic would last,
and not knowing what the future would bring. The
Jogger hadn't forgotten about her interesting run,
but life took over and she hadn't managed to go for
another run since. The plan to run more regularly
had been put aside, like many of her other plans to
live a healthier life.

Walking to her car as she headed out to do some
grocery shopping, the Jogger spotted Bill attending to
his Austin Cambridge as usual – waving to any and
every passer-by, curious as ever about other people's
days. Bill looked up from his waxing and polishing,
smiling when he saw the Jogger. His beaming face
seemed to shine even brighter today. Smiling back
as she made a beeline towards him, the Jogger now
welcomed conversations with Bill.

BILL: Good morning to you!

THE JOGGER: Morning, Bill. How are you?

BILL: I'm doing well, thank you. And what about you? What's been better for you lately?

The Jogger smiled warmly.

THE JOGGER: Not a whole lot, Bill. This pandemic is still creating chaos, but we're working our way through it. We're keeping ourselves busy with the kids, as you can imagine.

BILL: OK, so that's how things have been. And what has been better since our little chat when you were out running?

She wasn't surprised in the least to see that Bill was asking his questions again.

THE JOGGER: What's been better? A lot of what we talked about has started happening, now that I think about it. I'm way less worried now and far more relaxed about things.

BILL: That's brilliant. Tell me more. What has being far more relaxed looked like for you?

THE JOGGER: Well, I don't know if you knew, but I was feeling so overwhelmed by the current pressures and uncertainty that I was having panic attacks on a regular basis. And I'm happy to say I haven't had one since I went out for that run.

BILL: Wow, that's great! And what have you

been doing that's helped to make that happen?

THE JOGGER: It might sound too simple, but I've focused on what I wanted to do more of – like being with my family. We're doing more things together now. We're all working as a team to look after our garden properly, planting some veg, trimming back the bushes, and we might even returf the lawn, given how much time the kids spend out there at the moment. We've even built a little hideout together. It's been fun for all of us.

BILL: I've heard you all out in the garden, and it definitely sounds like you're having fun! What have you been seeing from your children and your partner that tells you they've been having fun too?

THE JOGGER: The kids have been laughing more and mostly getting along with each other, and they've been getting involved with the digging and planting. It's been great. As for my partner, he hasn't said very much.

BILL: Oh, come on, you two have been together for how long? Even if he hasn't said much, what have you noticed about him that shows he's having fun?

THE JOGGER: He's been in the garden with us instead of sitting in front of the TV, and he's the one that insisted on the hideout. He's been playing with the kids more as well.

BILL: Great. And how have you been reacting to him doing all those things?

THE JOGGER: It encourages me to get more involved. And I've been laughing more too. What about you, Bill? What's been better for you since we last met?

BILL: Oh, thank you for asking! I managed to get my old bicycle out of the garage and go for a ride, like my wife and I used to when she was still with me. That brought back some lovely memories, and I realised again how lucky I am to have lived them. So, a lot has been better!

THE JOGGER: That's great to hear.

BILL: Thanks, but anyway, back to you. Seeing your kids getting along with each other – what difference has that made to you and your partner?

THE JOGGER: It's not all rosy. We still have no idea what the future holds, but it makes us feel like we must be doing something right. Our family is happy together. That gives me hope that we will make the most of whatever comes next.

BILL: Aha, and there it is again – hope!

THE JOGGER: True. Thanks for asking about what's been better. If you hadn't asked, I wouldn't have looked for it. Good to see you again, Bill.

BILL: Good to see you too. And it's always worth looking out for what's been better!

And as she returned to her car, the Jogger realised

just how much had changed. She felt a renewed presence in the world around her and a sense of confidence, trust and hope. Things were more than OK. It was good to be alive.

Activity/Exercise:

Think of something you've been working towards for a while.

> What's been better since you started working towards it?

It's a tricky question. Intuitively, you might catch yourself thinking what's been worse or thinking no progress has been made at all. While there's a slim chance this might be true, we tend to find what we purposefully look for. So ...

> What's been better? Even by a little bit? Even if it seems not worth mentioning?

Then let's expand this:

> List ten ways in which this little thing that's been better has made a difference.

> Then list ten ways in which you have contributed to this improvement.

> After that, list five skills you've used that were useful.

And five ways that you have used each of those five skills.

In the end, you will have fifty different yet interconnected ways of how things have been better for you.

We can go on with this:

List five people who have noticed that things have been better for you, even by a little.

Then list five signs that told you they have noticed and what difference this has made to you.

After that, list ten things those people know about you that would give them trust you can continue your journey in the way that is right for you.

And fifteen things you know about yourself that give you trust and confidence you can continue your journey in the way that is right for you and those around you.

EPILOGUE

What's Next?

As you're reading this, we have no idea what the current circumstances will be. What we do know is that you will have been through numerous lockdowns, at least two waves of the coronavirus and an unimaginable number of changes to your life since the pandemic started. Just like our Jogger, you have made it through these uncertain times. Undoubtedly you will have learned a lot about yourself, adapted and perhaps even developed new skills. You're still here and you are finding ways to continue to move forward and make the best of life, regardless of COVID-19. So here is one final exercise for you to think about – to celebrate your abilities and achievements so far, as well as to reflect on the things you're already doing that are helpful and that will continue to serve you well, whatever the future holds.

Activity/Exercise:

Thinking about everything you have been through in this pandemic, what have you learned about yourself so far that gives you hope and confidence that you'll be able to manage whatever comes next?

Which existing skills, abilities and resources have you used along the way?

What skills and abilities have you developed during this time?

What difference does it make to you, knowing you have those skills and abilities?

Which of those skills and abilities would you like to develop further and take forward into the future? What impact would they make?

APPENDIX

ABOUT
THE SOLUTION-
FOCUSED APPROACH

**Solution-Focused – a different way of supporting
people on their journeys**

You might have wondered where these ideas,
questions and exercises come from, and whether
there's something more to it than just an interesting
tale of the Jogger's day.

As you travel through life, you will have the
privilege of meeting others on their important life
journeys. Some will be taking their first few steps;
others may have already travelled further than they
thought. Like the Jogger looking for clarity and
direction from friendly passers-by, we all seek help
and guidance. The question is: what is it that we can
do for ourselves and to support others?

It might be assumed that in order to be of help
to someone like the Jogger, we would need to
jog alongside them, try to understand them and
empathise with what it's like to be in their shoes. Or
we might need to help the Jogger plan her route, by
suggesting which turns she needs to take and which
checkpoints she needs to reach.

In truth, the people our Jogger meets do neither

of these things; instead, they concentrate on asking her to point her own way, showing curiosity as to what her desired destination is like, where her hopes are present and reminding her of her inner backpack. In a nutshell, allow us to briefly walk you through the Solution-Focused approach. It is a simple yet powerful approach to create change, and for the Jogger's journey, we have borrowed some of its basic principles. It can be a useful framework that will help you if you want to act as a counterpart on other Joggers' journeys, or indeed your own.

1. Pointing your way – not us, but you

The intention behind this is for the Jogger to end up pointing the way, rather than the passer-by. Sometimes we might expect the opposite, with the Jogger asking, 'Which direction do I need to go?' and the passer-by pointing towards a well-trodden path, assuming this Jogger wants to get to the same place via the same route as everyone else who comes past in running gear. In the Solution-Focused way of doing things, however, the passer-by would likely respond with, 'I don't know, you tell me.'

This is not to make it difficult for the Jogger, nor is it not wanting to help, but rather an acknowledgement that nobody but the Jogger herself is the true expert on the nature of her journey. It would be wrong of the passer-by to assume that they know where the Jogger wants to head or what route she needs to take. Assuming what somebody wants or needs in our talking with them is like pointing the

128

Jogger down a 10-kilometre urban running route without stopping to discover that she was actually hoping for a 5-kilometre woodland trail.

In the same way, Solution-Focused passers-by start the conversation by ascertaining the Jogger's desired direction of travel and what she is hoping to aim for, be that happiness, peace, courage, better friendships, more focus, or something else. We call this the Jogger's 'best hopes', and it is an important stage of the process, since knowing what the Jogger wants points the direction for the rest of the conversation. Specifically, we are looking for the presence of something that the Jogger wants, not the absence of something they do not want. The latter would only be as useful as a signpost stating 'Don't go that way,' while not actually telling you which direction to take.

Try asking: what are your best hopes from this conversation/this situation/our talking together? (Like Bill asked the Jogger in Chapter 2.)

2. Generating hope and injecting energy for their preferred future

The intention behind this stage of the Solution-Focused conversation is to invite the Jogger to tell us what her hopes look like. Rather than simply ascertaining the direction of the journey, stating a few pleasantries and waving goodbye, the passer-by in a Solution-Focused context shows genuine, in-depth curiosity about the Jogger's destination – her preferred future.

Initially, this curiosity might take her by surprise; she might not have expected the friendly passer-by to ask, 'So what will your destination look like?' There is a good chance, however, that her excitement and enthusiasm for reaching her destination will rise and rise as she describes it. The more detail she goes into, the lighter her feet will feel, the path will look a little straighter, and her energy will be a little greater.

In Solution-Focused work, this detailed description of where the Jogger wants to get to is called the 'preferred future'. Through questions about context (times and locations), interactions (between family members and friends), and activities (what the Jogger would be doing), the Solution-Focused practitioner facilitates the creation of a 'home for possibilities' – a world where the Jogger can experience, through description, imagination, thought and language, a future that fits well for her. Just as she was energised by a renewed sense of where she was heading, so the people you want to support might be motivated to start taking steps towards the desired future they have described.

Try asking: what would be the first sign that showed your hopes [insert your best hopes, as discovered and defined earlier] had been achieved? (Like the dog walker asked the Jogger in Chapter 3.)

3. Reminding them of their backpack of forgotten resources

The intention behind this stage of the Solution-Focused process is for the Jogger to be reminded of all the potential tools and resources she is carrying with her. Again, this might initially come across as a strange thing to enquire about, but the passer-by, if operating from a Solution-Focused perspective, would be interested in the Jogger's backpack.

It might be, for example, that the Jogger has a powerful torch, first-aid kit, waterproof jacket, map, compass, a change of socks, sandwiches, fruit, and hidden in a side pocket, a forgotten flapjack – all of which may prove useful for the remainder of her journey. By showing interest and asking about her backpack, the passer-by has potentially reminded the Jogger of the resources she is already carrying and the various uses for them.

In the same way that the metaphors of eating a sandwich, checking a map or changing into clean socks could make the Jogger's journey more comfortable and achievable, so can remembering personal qualities, attributes, skills and achievements. Solution-Focused practitioners often refer to these as 'resources' or 'instances of success' and deliberately ask questions that highlight them. The Jogger may be asked to recall times when she was at her best, when she overcame challenges, and when she managed to cope. All such occasions require qualities, skills and attributes, and these are the items in her metaphorical backpack.

Try asking: when was the last time your hopes were present in some way, even a little? How did you contribute to making that happen? (Like the hiker asked the Jogger in chapter 5.)

4. Intentional encouragement without leaving a footprint

By the time the Jogger has clarified her hopes, described them and reminded herself of what is in her backpack, our hope as Solution-Focused practitioners is that she will be in a better position to complete her journey. Hopefully, she will also appreciate the helpful, if unusual, conversation with a friendly passer-by.

At Solution Focused Possibilities, we believe that our intention behind the questions we ask is just as important as the questions themselves. Therefore, we are cheering you on in finding your own unique language and style for encouraging all Joggers, yourself included, to point their own way, showing curiosity about their destination, and reminding them of their backpack.

ACKNOWLEDGEMENTS

Ben, Biba and Greg would like to thank the following people, without whom this book would not be possible: Chris Iveson, Harvey Ratner and Evan George from BRIEF for the training, encouragement and challenge. Wendy Beeton-Townshend, Simon Burns and all the amazing colleagues from Bedford Borough Early Help for continuing to innovate in a Solution-Focused way and value the hopes of families and young people. Sue Lancaster and colleagues in the D-BIT service at Essex County Council, whose names we could fill this book with, for holding their nerve with Solution-Focused practice and providing a cutting-edge service to families.

All the practitioners who have attended our 'COVID Catch-ups' training and events – helping us to continue co-creating and sharpening our practice.

Jacob Adams for putting in countless hours reviewing our work and reminding us to 'show and not tell'.

Anna Swan for always helping us make each draft better than the last.

Michael Coates for an excellent proofread.

Nick Ellwood for the illustrations that brought our characters to life.

All the front-line workers who have kept hope alive during this challenging time. And our families for their incredible patience and support.

Most importantly, thank you to our clients for

continuing to inspire us with stories of resilience and transformation through even the darkest of times.

Ben, Biba and Greg are driven by a common passion: the hopefulness, simplicity and humility of the Solution-Focused approach. Their contrasting personalities and complementary styles brought them together to form Solution Focused Possibilities in 2019. They are committed to inspiring others (like you) and continuing the great work and principles of BRIEF, where they all trained. This means working in a constructive and minimalistic way, while continuing to reflect, explore and innovate.

Discover more at:
    www.sfpossibilities.org
    info@sfpossibilities.org

About the Authors

Ben Scott

Ben has been utilising solution-focused practice in an Early Help and Intervention setting since 2015. He delivers training to social workers, early-help practitioners and voluntary sector staff, led a solution-focused service for schools, and helps co-ordinate a bi-monthly 'SF community of practice'. Ben also works with Azalea, a charity helping women and men escape sexual exploitation.

   ben@sfpossibilities.org

Greg Oberbeck

Since 2012, Greg has been a Solution-Focused practitioner working with families as part of a team within social care in Essex. He is responsible for continued practice development, as well as providing solution-focused training across the organisation. He also works with the Young Women's Trust, and is an accreditor for the UK Association for Solution Focused Practice.

greg@sfpossibilities.org

A. Biba Rebolj

Biba started training other professionals only a year after her first solution-focused course in 2014, working in her home country, Slovenia, and later across the world. She is a keynote speaker at international conferences, a board member of the *Journal of Solution Focused Practices* and a lead trainer in Erasmus+ programmes, as well as specialising in group work for youths and youth workers.

biba@sfpossibilities.org